More Praise for

THE **RAGE** OF A PRIVILEGED CLASS

"Passionate and incisive...*Rage* is a riveting tool of instruction: It gives whites an insightful and honest look at what their black colleagues face daily and how they feel about it. Through interviews with scores of successful African-Americans, ranging from law partners to psychologists to college professors, he gives voice to a truth that most black professionals already know but that few whites believe or understand: Despite the tremendous gains of blacks, race does matter....For middle-class blacks, *Rage* is an affirmation and eloquent articulation of what are often confusing and conflicting emotions. For whites, *Rage* offers insight into a pain they may never have known existed."   —*Houston Chronicle*

"Cose's book ratchets up the discussion to a new level, revealing the frustrations and anger of middle-class blacks. The destructive impact racism has had on the black poor is a well-documented cancer of the American soul. But little has been written about its lingering effects on blacks who have escaped the ghetto for the better life that middle-class status is supposed to bring. Their hidden rage is a ticking time bomb that must be defused. But first it has to be understood. Cose's book offers readers that understanding."   —*USA Today*

"Drawing upon studies dealing with racial attitudes and a variety of experiences shared by members of the black elite, ranging from lawyers to executives to journalists, Cose's thoughtful and at times moving treatise makes the case that no matter how far a black person advances, that person will still be seen first and foremost as black, as opposed to just being a successful individual."   —*Boston Globe*

"Cose addresses the stress-inducing 'demons' he sees blacks coping with at work. These include a presumption of failure, an inability to fit in and guilt by association; they prompt him to call out the assumption 'that blacks are still on probation.'... Always convincing, clear-headed and fair-minded."
—*Cleveland Plain Dealer*

"*The Rage of a Privileged Class* is a probing scholarly portrayal of the vulnerability and victimization of many middle-class blacks, a condition shared by African-Americans in general. Nowhere is Cose more convincing than when he explores the double standards of a color-struck America. This is vividly illustrated when he contrasts the pejorative connotation of affirmative action, as applied to blacks, with the absence of insult when whites benefit from special programs or special consideration."
—*Christian Science Monitor*

"What Cose's book brings home is that the barriers of caste can be just as brutal in air-conditioned offices as on inner-city streets—all the more so when we are talking about people who have paid their dues."
—*The Nation*

"*Rage* is an ambitious and timely endeavor that alludes to the absence of any riches at the end of the rainbow. The author's pointed insight and analysis of race as the all-determining factor of achievement in the United States rings with an unrefutable truth. This book is a warning that dissatisfaction of the Black 'privileged class' must not be ignored. Dissent and the impetus for major social change may be stirring in the most unexpected of places."
—*Emerge*

"*The Rage of a Privileged Class* is a thoughtful and closely argued essay on race in America. By exploring the minds and hearts of the Black middle class, Cose addresses some of today's most urgent and vital issues of racial fairness and economic equality and courageously opens the door for honest, realistic dialogue."
—*Black Media News*

THE *RAGE*

OF A PRIVILEGED CLASS

ELLIS COSE

 HarperPerennial

A Division of HarperCollins*Publishers*

A hardcover edition of this book was published in 1993 by HarperCollins Publishers.

THE RAGE OF A PRIVILEGED CLASS. Copyright © 1993 by Ellis Cose. All rights reserved. Printed in the United States of America. No part of this book may be used or reproduced in any manner whatsoever without written permission except in the case of brief quotations embodied in critical articles and reviews. For information address HarperCollins Publishers, Inc., 10 East 53rd Street, New York, NY 10022.

HarperCollins books may be purchased for educational, business, or sales promotional use. For information please write: Special Markets Department, HarperCollins Publishers, Inc., 10 East 53rd Street, New York, NY 10022.

First HarperPerennial edition published 1995.

Designed by Barbara DuPree Knowles

The Library of Congress has catalogued the hardcover edition as follows:

Cose, Ellis.
    The rage of a privileged class / Ellis Cose.
        p.   cm.
    ISBN 0-06-018239-3
    1. Afro-Americans—Social conditions—1975– . 2. Middle classes—
United States. 3. United States—Social conditions—1980– . 4. United
States—Race relations. I. Title.
E185.86.C5883   1993
305.896´073—dc20   93-33202

ISBN 0-06-092594-9 (pbk.)

00 01 RRD   10   9   8

For Gwendolyn Brooks,
who inspired a teenaged writer to dream of greatness

contents

acknowledgments

Exposing one's private thoughts to public debate can be difficult, especially when those thoughts reveal a considerable amount of despair. Yet had it not been for the willingness of the men and women I interviewed to share their experiences and innermost feelings, this book could not have been written. I am deeply in their debt.

I am also indebted to my agent, Michael Congdon, for his ideas and encouragement; to editors Ed Burlingame, Aaron Asher, and Joy Johannessen for their enthusiastic support; and to Lee Llambelis, my wife, muse, and sometime critic, who believed in this book when it was merely a notion, and believed in me always. Finally, I thank Keith Campbell for helping me to keep my facts straight, while I reserve the right to claim all mistakes for myself.

Introduction: *Shouts and Whispers*

ESPITE ITS VERY EVIDENT PROSPERITY, MUCH of America's black middle class is in excruciating pain. And that distress—although most of the country does not see it—illuminates a serious American problem: the problem of the broken covenant, of the pact ensuring that if you work hard, get a good education, and play by the rules, you will be allowed to advance and achieve to the limits of your ability.

Again and again, as I spoke with people who had every accouterment of success, I heard the same plaintive declaration—always followed by various versions of an unchanging and urgently put question. "I have done everything I was supposed to do. I have stayed out of trouble with the law, gone to the right schools, and worked myself nearly to death. *What more do they want?* Why in God's name won't they accept me as a full human being? Why am I pigeonholed in a 'black job'? Why am I constantly treated as if I were a drug addict, a thief, or a thug? Why am I still not allowed to aspire to the same things every white person in America takes as a birthright? Why, when I most want to be seen, am I suddenly rendered invisible?"

What exactly do such questions mean? Could their underlying premise conceivably be correct? Why, a full generation after the most celebrated civil rights battles were fought and won, are Americans still struggling with basic issues of racial fairness? This book attempts to provide some possible answers. And in exploring why so many of those who have invested most deeply in the American dream are consumed with anger and pain, I hope to

1

show how certain widespread and amiable assumptions held by whites—specifically about the black middle class but also about race relations in general—are utterly at odds with the reality many Americans confront daily.

That the black middle class (and I use the term very loosely, essentially meaning those whose standard of living is comfortable, even lavish, by most reasonable measures) should have any gripes at all undoubtedly strikes many as strange. The civil rights revolution, after all, not only killed Jim Crow but brought blacks more money, more latitude, and more access to power than enjoyed by any previous generation of African Americans. Some blacks in this new era of opportunity have amassed fortunes that would put Croesus to shame. If ever there was a time to celebrate the achievements of the color-blind society, now should be that time.

Joe Feagin, a sociologist at the University of Florida, observed in a paper prepared for the U.S. Commission on Civil Rights that most whites believe that blacks no longer face significant racial barriers. "From this white perspective employment discrimination targeting black Americans is no longer a serious problem in the United States. The black middle class, in particular, has largely overcome job discrimination and is thriving economically. Only the black underclass is in serious trouble, and that has little to do with discrimination." Indeed, many people believe the tables have turned so far that whites are more likely to be victimized by discrimination than blacks.

At an early stage of my work, I outlined the thesis of this book to Daniel Patrick Moynihan, senior senator from New York and celebrated scholar of ethnicity. Moynihan made the counterargument succinctly. The black middle class, he noted, was "moving along very well." And he had every expectation that it would continue to do so. Indeed, with so many black mayors and black police chiefs in place, blacks represented, to many new arrivals, America's power establishment. "The big problem," added Moynihan, "is, 'What are we going to do about the underclass?' And a particular problem is that [the] black group you're talking about [the middle class] doesn't want to have anything to do with them."

Certainly one can show statistically that black "married-couple families" with wives in the paid labor force (as categorized by the U.S. Census Bureau) do not make *that* much less than comparably stratified whites. Such households, which earn slightly over 80 percent as much as similar white households, are arguably within striking distance of economic parity. One can empathize with Moynihan's pique when he reflects on the public reaction to his famous 1970 memorandum to Richard Nixon pointing out that young two-parent black families in the Northeast were progressing nicely and suggesting that perhaps race could benefit from a period of "benign neglect." "I went through hell's own time," recalls Moynihan.

But whatever such aggregate statistics may show, they do not demonstrate—and cannot—that hiring has become color-blind. As Andrew Hacker observes in *Two Nations*, "While there is now a much larger black middle class, more typically, the husband is likely to be a bus driver earning $32,000, while his wife brings home $28,000 as a teacher or a nurse. A white middle-class family is three to four times more likely to contain a husband earning $75,000 in a managerial position." Feagin notes that he has found *"no* [emphasis his] research study with empirical data supporting the widespread white perspective that employment discrimination is no longer serious in the U.S. workplace."

In lieu of scientific research, we are offered speculation and conjecture, self-congratulatory theories from whites who have never been forced to confront the racial stereotypes routinely encountered by blacks, and who—judging themselves decent people, and judging most of their acquaintances decent as well—find it impossible to believe that serious discrimination still exists. Whatever comfort such conjecture may bring some whites, it has absolutely no relevance to the experiences of blacks in America.

I am not suggesting that most whites are "racist." The majority emphatically are not—at least not in any meaningful sense of the word. If a racist is defined as one who hates blacks (or members of any other racial group, for that matter), the number of true racists is very small, and a substantial portion of them are the pathetic sorts of people who call themselves Nazis and glorify the

Ku Klux Klan. Even those fanatics tend to be motivated less by racism than by some pathology expressed in racial terms. The point here, however, is that people do not have to be racist—or have any malicious intent—in order to make decisions that unfairly harm members of another race. They simply have to do what comes naturally.

In 1991, ABC's "Primetime Live" attempted to gauge the effect of race on average black and white Americans. Over a period of two and a half weeks, the program followed two "testers," one black and one white, both trained to present themselves in an identical manner in a variety of situations. At times, host Diane Sawyer acknowledged, the two men were treated equally, but over and over—"every single day," she said—they were not.

The white tester, John, got instant service at an electronics counter; the black one, Glenn, was ignored. Glenn was tailed, not helped, by the salesman in a record store, while John was allowed to shop on his own. Passersby totally ignored Glenn when he was locked out of his car; John was showered with offers of help. In an automobile showroom, Glenn was quoted a price of $9,500 (with a 20 to 25 percent down payment) for the same red convertible offered to John for $9,000 (with a 10 to 20 percent down payment). In an apartment complex, John was given the keys to look around, while Glenn was told that the apartment was rented. At an employment agency, Glenn was lectured on laziness and told he would be monitored "real close," while John was treated with consideration and kindness. At a dry cleaners, Glenn was turned down flat for a job and John was encouraged to apply. In encounter after encounter, the subtle insults and rejections that Glenn had to swallow mounted, to the extent that even the two professional testers said their eyes had been opened.

"Primetime Live" did its experiment in St. Louis, Missouri. Yet throughout America, black and white Johns and Glenns, no matter how equivalent their backgrounds and personal attributes, live fundamentally different lives. And because the experiences are so immensely different, even for those who walk through the same institutions, it is all but impossible for members of one group to see the world through the other's eyes. That lack of a common perspective often translates into a lack of empathy, and an inability on the part of most whites to perceive, much less understand, the soul-destroying slights at the heart of black middle-class discontent.

This is not to say that white Americans are intent on persecuting black people, or that blacks are utterly helpless and fault-free victims of society. Nothing could be further from the truth. Nonetheless, America is filled with attitudes, assumptions, stereotypes, and behaviors that make it virtually impossible for blacks to believe that the nation is serious about its promise of equality—even (perhaps especially) for those who have been blessed with material success.

Donald McHenry, former U.S. permanent representative to the United Nations, told me that though he felt no sense of estrangement himself, he witnessed it often in other blacks who had done exceptionally well: "It's sort of the in talk, the in joke, within *the club*, an acknowledgment of and not an acceptance . . . of the effect of race on one's life, on where one lives, on the kinds of jobs that one has available. I think that's always been there. I think it's going to be there for some time." Dorothy Gilliam, a columnist for the *Washington Post*, expressed a similar thought in much stronger terms. "You feel the rage of people, [of] your group . . . just being the dogs of society."

Upon declaring her intention to leave a cushy job with a Fortune 500 company to go into the nonprofit sector, a young black woman, a Harvard graduate, was pulled aside by her vice president. Why, the executive wanted to know, was the company having such a difficult time retaining young minority professionals? The young woman's frustrations were numerous: she felt herself surrounded by mediocrity, by people trying to advance on the basis of personal influence and cronyism rather than merit; she was weary of racial insensitivity, of people who saw nothing about her except her color, or conversely of those who, in acknowledging her talents, in effect gave her credit for not really being black; she deemed it unlikely, given her perceptions of the corporate culture, that she would be allowed to make it to the top, and feared waking up in a rut several years hence to find that opportunities (and much of life) had passed her by; and she was tired of having to bite her tongue, tired of feeling that she could only speak out about the wrongs she perceived at the risk of being labeled a malcontent and damaging her career. Rather than try to explain, the woman finally blurted out that there was "no one who looks like me" in all of senior management—by which she meant there were no blacks, and certainly no black women. "What reason do I have to believe," she added, "that *I* can make it to the top?" When she related the incident to me several years later, she remained discouraged by what seemed a simple reality of her existence. "The bottom line is you're black. And that's still a negative in this society."

Ulric Haynes, dean of the Hofstra University School of Business and a former corporate executive who served as President Carter's ambassador to Algeria, is one of many blacks who have given up hope that racial parity will arrive this—or even next— millennium: "During our lifetimes, my children's lifetimes, my grandchildren's lifetimes, I expect that race will . . . matter. And perhaps race will always matter, given the historical circumstances under which we came to this country." But even as he recognizes that possibility, Haynes is far from sanguine about it. In fact, he is angry. "Not for myself. I'm over the hill. I've reached the zenith," he says. "I'm angry for the deception that this has perpetrated on my children and grandchildren." Though his children have traveled the world and received an elite education, they "in a very real sense are not the children of privilege. They are dysfunctional, because I didn't prepare them, in all the years we lived overseas, to deal with the climate of racism they are encountering right now."

In 1992, a research team at UCLA's Center for the Study of Urban Poverty benefited from a fortuitous accident of timing. They were midway through the field work for a survey of racial attitudes in Los Angeles County when a jury exonerated four white policemen of the most serious charges in the videotaped beating of a black man named Rodney King. The riot that erupted in South Central Los Angeles in the aftermath of the verdict delayed the researchers' work, so they ended up, in effect, with two surveys: one of attitudes before the riot, and one of attitudes after.

The questionnaire they used included four statements thought to be helpful in measuring "ethnic alienation from American Society": "American Society owes people of my ethnic group a better chance in life than we currently have." "American society has provided people of my ethnic group a fair opportunity to get ahead in life." "I am grateful for the special opportunities people of my ethnic group have found in America." "American society just hasn't dealt fairly with people from my background."

Responses to the statements were merged into a single score, cataloged by income level and ethnic group. The responses of blacks with a household income of $50,000 and more were especially intriguing. Even before the riot, that group, on average, appeared to be more alienated than poorer blacks. But what stunned the researchers was that after the riot, alienation among the most affluent group of African Americans skyrocketed, rising nearly a full "standard deviation"—much more than it did for those who were less well off. In reporting the findings, the UCLA team wrote: "This strong and uniform rise in black alienation from American social institutions is the single clearest and most consistent change observed from any of the items we have examined. Careful inspection of responses shows that this rising discontent occurred among black men and women, as well as across educational and income levels. With respect to the effects of income level, however, there is an unexpected twist. . . . Analysis of this 'Ethnic Alienation from American Society' measure showed, critically, that the rise in discontent was strongest among black households whose incomes were $50,000 or higher." The researchers concluded: "Our own data strongly confirm that middle class blacks continue to feel the burdens of discrimination."

In a press release, Lawrence Bobo, a UCLA sociologist who directed the survey, added, "These are people of high accomplishment and who have worked hard for what they have achieved. As far as they are concerned, however, what happened to Rodney

King can just as easily befall any of them. Given all the dues they have paid, and all the contributions the black middle class has made, these events—especially the jury verdict—came as a jolt of racial injustice.''

It's quite possible that the leap in alienation recorded by Bobo and company was an ephemeral phenomenon, nothing more than a passing wave of anger generated by an extraordinary event. The entire country, after all, seemed in a state of shock over the verdict in Simi Valley. But that does not account for the sentiments registered before the verdict, when so many blacks who were doing well seemed to be so very unhappy. So many seemed in a state of raging discontent. And much of America, I am sure, has not a ghost of a notion why.

In the pages that follow, individuals of substantial accomplishment explain why they are angry. In some cases, they have given up hope that the covenant will ever be honored. Others hold on to the dream that it eventually will. What they have to say will surprise those who assume that the black middle class has it made. But even many who admit the legitimacy of the complaints will be disinclined to care. For the problems of the black middle class, they will argue, pale by comparison with those of the underclass, the group that truly deserves our attention.

That response would be a grave mistake. Formidable though the difficulties of the so-called underclass are, America can hardly afford to use the plight of the black poor as an excuse for blinding itself to the difficulties of the black upwardly mobile. For one thing, though the problems of the two classes are not altogether the same, they are in some respects linked. Moreover, one must at least consider the possibility that a nation which embitters those struggling hardest to believe in it and work within its established systems is seriously undermining any effort to provide would-be hustlers and dope dealers with an attractive alternative to the streets. But whatever one believes about the relative merits of the grievances expressed by the different economic classes, clearly the troubles of one do not cancel out the concerns of the other.

Obviously, blacks are not America's only group still wrestling with how—or whether—to fit into the mainstream. Hispanics,

Asians, and other ethnic minorities, as well as women, also experience stereotyping and chauvinism. Others claim bias because of sexual orientation or age. And increasingly, even young straight white men see themselves as victims of discrimination. (A national survey of American youth conducted in 1991 by Peter Hart Research Associates found whites more likely to believe that "qualified whites" were hurt by affirmative action than that "qualified minorities" were harmed by racial discrimination.) The histories and current experiences of all these groups differ too much to lump them together in one coherent analysis. In focusing on the predicament of blacks, and specifically of those who belong to the middle class, I do not intend to imply that the concerns of others are trivial, or that there are no similarities between their situation and that of blacks, or no common lessons to be divined. In reality, the opposite is true.

Yet even in this age of "diversity" and multiculturalism, the status of blacks in American society rates special attention. No other racial group in America's history has endured as much rejection on the path to acceptance. No other group has stared so longingly and for so long at what Sharon Collins, a University of Illinois sociologist, calls "the final door." And no other group remains so uncertain of admittance.

Racial discussions tend to be conducted at one of two levels—either in shouts or in whispers. The shouters are generally so twisted by pain or ignorance that spectators tune them out. The whisperers are so afraid of the sting of truth that they avoid saying much of anything at all.

Those profiled in the following pages are neither shouting nor whispering. They are trying, in a more honest manner than is generally encouraged, to explain how race affects their lives and the lives of those they care about. They are passionately, often eloquently, sometimes anonymously bearing witness. Their hope—and mine—is that their voices will be heard.

chapter one *Why Successful People Cry the Blues*

◆◆◆◆◆◆◆◆◆◆◆◆◆◆◆◆◆◆◆◆◆◆◆◆◆◆◆◆◆◆

IN OCTOBER 1992, EDWARD KOCH, THE FORMER mayor of New York, delivered what was billed as a major lecture on race at New York University. I opted not to attend, largely because I couldn't imagine that Koch, given what seemed to be a tin ear for racial harmonics, could do the subject justice. Nonetheless, when he sent me—and, I'm sure, a long list of others—a copy of his remarks along with a note calling race and its impact on society "the most important subject facing the United States," I was seized with curiosity.

I found that instead of dwelling on polarizing sentiments of the sort he had been identified with in the past, Koch had produced a serious and thoughtfully nuanced essay. In it, he documented—and strongly denounced—widespread, continuing racial discrimination, discussing with sensitivity and insight the indignities American society imposes on "the individual black . . . every day of his or her life."

But racism, he insisted, was not a permanent feature of American life and could eventually be licked—though not through quotas, and not until black violence was dealt with honestly, and not as long as so many black and Hispanic youths were "disaffiliated from society." Koch proposed to combat such disaffection through universal national service that would compel everyone temporarily to relocate and thereby "take those who . . . are disaffiliated out of their environment." He also spoke in favor of more education and employment training programs, and more federal jails. And he issued a blunt and passionate call to put "facts above preconception": "Because we are not willing to face up to the importance of who we are and where we come from, we will never have the candid dialogue and the real debate we should have."

I spoke with Koch shortly after reading his speech, and he told me he had worked extremely hard on it. I said I thought it showed, and that though I disagreed with some of his opinions and prescriptions, I emphatically agreed with what I took to be his central point, that Americans are afraid to talk honestly about race. The reason for prevarication, to Koch, seemed quite apparent. Many whites fear that "if they talk honestly they'll be called a racist," while many blacks, he conjectured, were scared they'd be called Uncle Toms.

I told him I suspected blacks were less afraid of being called Uncle Toms than of being penalized for speaking out against racial inequities, and that his concept of universal service did not even begin to come to grips with the principal causes of alienation. Koch argued that unless I had a better solution, his was certainly worth a try, pointing to Israel and how it had taken in "one hundred and twenty different races and ethnic groups and . . . melded them into one nation."

While it's no doubt true that removing people from slums and placing them in a more wholesome environment could go a long way toward reducing crime (if only because it would expose some young delinquents to a more productive set of goals), it doesn't follow that it would do much to reduce alienation. Many well-educated, affluent blacks have already found their way out of inner-city ghettos, yet they have not escaped America's myriad racial demons. Consequently, they remain either estranged or in a state of emotional turmoil.

Even if black alienation *and* black crime could be lessened merely by putting young blacks into the American equivalent of kibbutzim, there is little reason to believe the result would be an end to discrimination against blacks. Notwithstanding currently fashionable arguments that blame white racism on black crime, it's unlikely that discrimination against certifiably "safe" blacks stems primarily from fear of black violence. Black executives, for instance, are not barred from private country clubs because white members fear their African-American peers will rob them. Nor do black associates in law firms have such difficulty advancing because white partners fear that black lawyers will rape their wives. Something other than anxiety over black crime is at work—something that lowering the black crime rate (desirable though that is) or even taking young blacks out of their environment (beneficial though that may be) will not necessarily change.

Edward W. Jones, a black management consultant who specializes in racial issues, agrees with Koch that an honest dialogue on race is urgently required, but he views the issue very differently from the former mayor. "If we think just education, middle-class values, and proper enunciation will be adequate, we're making a serious mistake," says Jones. The problem, as he sees it, is not merely (or even mostly) black attitudes, but those of whites who still retain so much power over black lives: "As a numerical minority . . . the only power we've really got is to be sure that we define the problem correctly."

One could argue *ad infinitum* over Jones's assessment of the limits of black power. What one cannot refute, however, is the reality of the perceptual chasm separating so many blacks and whites. The problem is not only that we are afraid to talk to one another, it is also that we are disinclined to listen. And even when the will to understand is present, often the ability (gained through analogous experiences) is not.

In some respects, the answer to "Why are these people so angry?" is not at all simple. For one thing, none are angry all the time. A few deny their anger even as they show it. And while all African Americans, in one way or another, have spent their lives coping with racial demons, the impact has not been identical. Some have been beaten into an almost numb submission, into accepting that they will never reach the goals they once thought possible. Others have refused to accept that being black means being treated as a lesser human being, and they respond to each insult with furious indignation. A number wonder whether, given the blessings they have received, they have any right to be angry at all.

The sketches that follow are offered not only to give a sense of why some middle-class blacks are angry, but to put that anger in the context of the hopes, fears, and insecurities that come with being human, irrespective of race.

The Trade Association Vice President

To the world, he presents a charming, self-assured facade, yet he often wonders whether his career is in a terminal stall. He has been with the trade association for more than a decade, having previously held an array of impressive-sounding jobs in sales, government, research, and marketing. But despite his experience, his law degree, his lofty title, and a personality that makes him a natural diplomat, he has been given responsibility for little more than "minority affairs."

It is an assignment, he acknowledges, that no one else in the organization wanted or "would care to be associated with." And though he accepted it enthusiastically, he has come to realize that the minority affairs portfolio is not one that will do him any good. The topic of progress for minorities, he is convinced, "conjures up feelings of confusion and guilt" among whites within his industry.

He did not reach that conclusion lightly, or even on his own. He was guided toward it largely by a former boss who, in a moment of comradely candor, told him why his career had run into a ditch. Though he did his job extremely well, the former boss said, no one really appreciated him: "When they look at you, they see black issues, problems. . . . They don't like what you do."

That his superiors considered his work unimportant had been clear to him all along. All other department heads regularly presented reports to the board of directors, but he had to plead for the privilege. His entire budget was smaller than the salaries of certain high-ranking executives in the association, and one-third that of the next smallest department. For years he had begged for additional assignments, but his entreaties had been spurned. The manager of government relations had refused, point blank, to work with him, citing the inviolability of turf. No other coworker had rejected him quite so bluntly, but word had gotten back that some felt he was too much a self-promoter. "They see you as having too much power, and they don't want to do any more to augment that," a friendly white colleague had told him. In response to such feedback, he had resolutely lowered his profile, sharply cutting back on speeches and participation in public events.

"I brought to this job a lot of experience," he gloomily observed, yet he now felt trapped in an unfulfilling role that tapped only a fraction of his potential. And he didn't see things changing for the better any time soon. In the old days, when black issues were in vogue, he felt he and his department had a certain amount of clout, or at least that he commanded "a sort of reluctant respect." He feared, however, that the industry no longer believed race relations to be a problem worthy of attention. And to make matters worse, he had stayed in his present job long enough and become so visible in it that he had been pigeonholed as an affirmative-action man.

"I would have been gone a long time ago," he confessed, but noted that the jobs he had thus far been offered either paid less or promised a similar set of frustrations. So he was resigned, for the present, to staying where he was as he tried to focus on the positive aspects of his situation. He had a decent salary, a good deal of autonomy, and a certainty that he was doing something worthwhile, despite the attitude of his employers.

Yet he could not help but feel dissatisfied and more than a little bit bitter; and at one point, during a lengthy conversation, he turned to me and asked, "Am I the only one who feels this way?"

The Partner

He is one of the nation's most successful lawyers, comfortably ensconced at a prestigious East Coast firm that would not even have granted him an interview when he graduated from law school some three decades ago. Back then, he had tried to get a Wall Street job but was told that despite his degree from a top-notch school and his appointment to the law review, Negroes were not hired as Wall Street lawyers. So he had gone to work for the federal government.

A few years later, after the civil rights revolution shook the nation, the private sector began to open up. In the late 1960s, major law firms began very tentatively to recruit blacks. "Everybody wanted one," he recalls. And he intended to take advantage of the shift in the winds. Moreover, he felt he understood the kind of attitude he had to demonstrate in order to get a job. "I knew white folks. I knew how to deal with them." He understood how to ask "nonconfrontational questions" and how to appear "calm and deliberate."

He talked to several firms. Many of the interviewers lied, denying that racism existed in their establishments, and concocting any number of excuses for not having employed blacks. But one firm was different. The partners acknowledged that they had discriminated in the past but said they were prepared to change and share power. He was impressed with their honesty and their general approach, but not without reservations. Through no fault of his own, he pointed out, he had been denied entry to a major law firm, and he did not want to be penalized for that. Provided he could prove his worth, he did not want to be kept on a string forever, but to be made a partner straightaway. They agreed, and he came aboard. The year was 1970.

For a while, struggling to adjust to the ways of the firm, he felt embarrassingly adrift. Having always worked for the government, he had no idea how to bill his time, and nobody volunteered to show him. So he resolved to figure it out on his own: "I would go in on Saturday and sneak into people's offices to see what in the fuck they were doing." He persevered and eventually prospered, largely, he believes, because he mastered an obvious and supremely important lesson: "If I was valuable to the bottom line, a lot of that racial shit would be overcome."

His court appearances were a source of pride, but also of annoyance. Though he generally did well, he sensed that he was not really seen as a litigator but as a *black* litigator. "I would go to court and do a workmanlike job, nothing special," and receive rave reviews, not only from colleagues but from judges. "They were impressed with me because their assumption was that I should have been dumb and ignorant." In that sense, he acknowledges, his color was probably an advantage: "Being black and competent, I had more visibility, and I got more credit."

His growing stature within the firm did not end his partners' racial insensitivity. They continued to hold important meetings at a private club that did not admit blacks unless they were accompanied by a member. Rather than do business in a place where he felt so unwelcome, he simply opted not to attend. Finally he was confronted by a Jewish partner who demanded to know the reason for his boycott. "I told him that going to that club was, for me, like going to a club that idolized Hitler would be for him." The partners eventually stopped meeting at the place, but he is convinced that the firm remains less than hospitable to blacks.

When he was made a partner, a little less than three years after signing up, his first act was to request his personnel file. What he saw astounded him and confirmed his impression that many factors considered relevant to partnership potential were idiotically idiosyncratic. He discovered that one partner, disapproving of his Afro hairstyle, had fretted over his "bushy" appearance. Another had worried that clients might not accept him. Yet another, noting that he had worked for a civil rights agency, wondered whether his politics might not be too radical.

At partnership meetings where the future of associates is determined, he still sees evidence of subjective criteria being used to weed blacks out. "Someone will say, 'Tom Jones is a wonderful lawyer. He really has a lot to offer. However . . .' One has to look out for the 'however.' I've seen them destroy people with the 'however.' " Too often, he says, the "however" is followed by criticisms like "he cannot perform *on a day to day basis*, or *at a certain level*," phrases that seem to say something but in reality say nothing at all. When he hears such comments directed at talented blacks, he makes a point of stopping the conversation to demand clarification. In so doing, he says, he can keep a career from being destroyed out of unconscious and unthinking prejudice: "By being there, I can prevent that from happening to a black associate. . . . Once you do that, people back off; but if you're not there . . . nobody's going to question this stuff."

Because such subtle discrimination continues, he worries

about his children and those of his black peers, for he believes they are inheriting a world that is in some respects more treacherous than the one in which he came of age. "In the sixties, you knew white people didn't like black folks," he says, but today things are not so clear. Consequently, raising children presents an extraordinary predicament. "You educate your kids with the hope they will be given a fair shot," which means shielding them from racial rejection. But the result is that they may not be ready for the "street fight" he is sure they will face in the white world: "This is the goddamn dilemma. And that is why I have this rage."

His views on racial progress in general have a distinctly pessimistic cast. He is convinced that a ceiling exists for most African Americans, that black skin is still equated by many in the business community with a lowering of standards, and that nothing much will change that. "I don't care how good blacks become. If blacks were all educated, all went to school, and all got the best grades . . . it wouldn't help us. It would probably increase our frustration."

For individual blacks, he sees some protection in "becoming valuable" by making money for the enterprise. But discrimination, he believes, will be a constant. "We fought some fights," he says, "but the kids are going to have to fight this fight again." He adds softly, almost prayerfully, "I don't want my kids to have to go through this shit."

The Journalist

Joel Dreyfuss is editor of *PC Magazine*, the nation's number-one publication for owners of personal computers. He is a man with a reputation for speaking his mind—a reputation that has not always served him well, in his view. His journalistic talent has landed him a host of impressive positions: reporter for the *Washington Post*, managing editor for *Black Enterprise*, New York bureau chief for *USA Today*, Tokyo bureau chief for *Fortune*. But an unfair perception of him as a racial rabble-rouser, he believes, has limited his success.

Dreyfuss, whose parents are Haitian, grew up shuttling among

Haiti, Africa, and the United States, in the tow of a father attached to the United Nations. He settled in New York, more or less for good, at the age of fifteen. When he enrolled in school, he found that despite his elite prior education, he was immediately "put in a class of basketball players." Shortly thereafter, he took an exam, and a counselor told him in apparent astonishment that he had done extremely well. He found the counselor's attitude bewildering, since until then he had always been expected to do well.

The reassessment of his abilities gained him entry to an honors program whose ethnic composition left him puzzled. In a school that was roughly 90 percent black and Hispanic, the honors program was 90 percent white. To all appearances, they had "created a school for white kids within the school." He entered City College of New York in the mid-1960s, before the open admissions policy, at a time when CCNY was considered one of the best schools in the city. The white students often asked him how he had managed to get in.

With the country caught up in the throes of rebellion, his interest in journalism blossomed. In addition to seeing journalism as force for social reform, he saw it as something of a family tradition; his father, years previously, had been publisher of an English-language paper in Haiti. Dreyfuss got a job at the Associated Press, where one evening, while helping to edit copy, he saw an AP story about three black men who had been accused of a crime. He questioned whether the racial identification was appropriate, citing AP policy prohibiting the use of racial designations unless they were somehow relevant to the story. The editor, in explaining why race was in fact relevant, asked, "Aren't blacks arming themselves?"

For Dreyfuss, the incident was a turning point. "I became outraged and I remained outraged for about twenty years." At that moment he realized that when faced with issues involving race, normally intelligent whites could become "irrational" and "would violate their own rules." He found support for that view a short while later when he went to work for the New York *Post*, where an editor involved in his hiring remarked, "Your people are trying to destroy us."

Such foolishness from editors fueled Dreyfuss's desire to seek change. He pushed his bosses to hire more blacks and criticized coverage he considered particularly witless. Not surprisingly, some found his outspokenness annoying, but his journalistic gifts nonetheless made him a standout. At the *Washington Post*, where Dreyfuss worked after leaving New York, an editor was so impressed that she took him aside to tell him that he was doing a terrific job. "How do we get more blacks as good as Joel Dreyfuss?" she asked. Dreyfuss found the remark offensive, and told her as much.

As a result of his propensity for rubbing editors the wrong way with his racial consciousness-raising, Dreyfuss was denied a coveted transfer to the California bureau. Ben Bradlee, then executive editor, acknowledged his abilities but told him that he was "a pain in the ass." The Bradlee kiss-off became a footnote in the Bradlee legend and cemented Dreyfuss's reputation as a troublemaker. For years after he left the *Post*, recalls Dreyfuss, the widely reported Bradlee remark "made it difficult for me to get a job in the mainstream media."

He tried, often at great emotional price, to live his reputation down, and learned to keep his mouth shut even when events outraged him. Yet nearly two decades after that episode, "there are still a lot of people who view me as a dangerous subversive. . . . I've been told that."

For all the pain the 1960s and '70s evoke, Dreyfuss believes they allowed certain black journalists to thrive. In those days, race was major story, and blacks were essential to covering that story. As a result, a fair number of black journalists became stars. Now he believes the best reporting jobs are largely going to whites, a reflection not only of the changing nature of the news, but of the fact that most news organizations still have "a limited imagination when it comes to black people."

The Law Professor

Anita Allen, a full professor at Georgetown University Law Center, is haunted by a sense that her life has been too easy. With her

Ph.D. in philosophy from the University of Michigan and her law degree from Harvard, she can match credentials with academia's best and brightest. Yet she knows that in some important respects her race has given her an edge—and a burden.

When going for her Ph.D. in the 1970s, she was admitted to several top schools, even though her Graduate Record Exam scores placed her closer to the eightieth percentile than to the ninety-eighth. And after she decided on Michigan, the Ford Foundation gave her a full fellowship, even though some of her white counterparts had to struggle to make ends meet. After receiving her doctorate, while many of her classmates were striving unsuccessfully to line up coveted interviews, she got more than her share and was hired by Carnegie Mellon University. Not that the offer was undeserved; she did, after all, graduate in the top 10 percent of her class. And not that the academic environment was always supportive. At one point, as a doctoral candidate and teaching fellow, she was confronted by a young white man who demanded to know, "What gives you the right to teach this class?" She assumed a similar challenge would not have been made had she been male and white. Indeed, the man who recruited her for Carnegie Mellon told her, in effect, that she would not have been hired had she been white. "I'm not sure you have the power we're looking for," she recalls him saying, in assessing her intellectual ability and drive.

She shrugged off the slight and threw herself into her work; but despite her popularity as a philosophy professor, she soon found herself experiencing "a sense of irrelevance." Law school, she decided, might be a ticket to "more meaningful work."

Like her graduate school exams, her law school boards were less than stellar, but she nonetheless won acceptance to Harvard. The law school curriculum was more difficult than her course work at Michigan, and her academic struggle was compounded by a sense of being subjected to heightened scrutiny, by what she calls "the pressure of being a black person under the microscope." The pressure became so intense that she suffered depression and migraine headaches, and her physician put her on antiseizure drugs.

Away from school, the race-related tension did not abate. On her first day as a summer associate at a Wall Street firm, she was asked to write a memo explaining why private clubs had a constitutional right to exclude women and minorities. When she expressed her disapproval of discrimination, the partner dismissed her objection as irrelevant, telling her he was not interested in "sociological considerations."

Despite the initial discomfort, she did well that summer, and after receiving her law doctorate, waltzed into a job with the tony white-shoe firm of Cravath, Swaine and Moore. Here, as at Carnegie Mellon, she was bluntly informed that she had not been hired for her intellectual firepower. The partner who offered her the position told her she had the worst grades he had ever seen but that she made up for this deficiency with her poise and articulateness.

"I've been a very lucky person," she says, without irony. She got a good education, thanks in large part to affirmative action, and she has been helped at many points along the way, perhaps more than her white counterparts. Not that she got something for nothing. She has always worked extremely hard, habitually showing up at work around seven in the morning and staying until late at night.

Moreover, she has faced heartache and hurdles at every step. When she and another lawyer at Cravath, Swaine were meeting with an important client, for instance, her colleague announced he had to leave early, but paused long enough to reassure the client about her abilities. She was hurt that he felt it necessary to do that—enough so that years later the incident stands out in her mind. She is unsure whether the gesture was a comment on her race, her gender, her youthfulness, or all three, but she attributed it to race. "Just a feeling I had," she says. Yet notwithstanding such minor humiliations, she always felt she could succeed at the firm. And she left of her own volition, having decided to give the academic track another try.

As a Georgetown law professor, she again absorbed racial blows. After addressing the American Association of University Professors on the issue of "discriminatory harassment on campuses," she found herself talking to a middle-aged white man who explained that she should not take offense at being called a jungle bunny because "you are cute and so are bunnies." On another occasion, a white scholar said she reminded him of his family's former maid. And once, "on a hot day in which I had my kinky hair tied back in a bandanna," wrote Allen in the *Berkeley Women's Law Journal*, "a white colleague innocently remarked that I looked like comedian Eddie Murphy's parody of [the 'Our Gang' television series character] Buckwheat." All the comments registered, all caused pain, but she feels that none of this boorishness really stood in her way.

After her fourth year at Georgetown, she was awarded tenure by a unanimous vote, strictly on the merits of her case, she believes. She estimates that she had produced the second highest number of publications of any member of the faculty, and as her colleagues were well aware, she was being pursued by law schools at Stanford, Michigan, Berkeley, and elsewhere. Eventually even Harvard came calling, and she accepted the invitation of Dean Robert Clark to be a visiting professor during the 1990–91 academic year.

In taking the offer, she was really consenting to an elaborate dance that would conclude with her appointment to the Harvard faculty if everything went well. The pressure was intense, and the dance was very public: Allen arrived shortly after Derrick Bell, renowned scholar and Harvard Law School's first black faculty member, announced that he was taking a leave of absence in protest, and would neither accept his $120,000 salary nor return to the school until a black woman was hired for the permanent faculty. Bell's ultimatum became a big story in the press and threw much of the Harvard community into turmoil.

Allen tried to concentrate on her work. After her stint was done, she returned to Georgetown, hopeful that she had performed well enough to be tapped for a permanent post. Instead, she got a call from a supporter at Harvard who suggested that her candidacy should probably be tabled until the political situation calmed down. It was. Shortly thereafter, she heard that Harvard had made offers to four white males.

"Not getting that job offer was the first time I had gone for something and I didn't get it," she says. And the fact that the rejection was so public made the pain much harder to take. She had always assumed the powers that be at Harvard were not merely playing a game, that they knew her and her record and would not have invited her if she did not stand a chance. She also knew that whatever insufficiencies they could find in her transcript, she had an outstanding professional track record. She had completed a book during her first year at Georgetown, and had both a doctorate in philosophy and a law degree. She could not understand Harvard's refusal to hire her, or even to accord her the courtesy of an official explanation. But neither is she sure she has much ground for complaint, only that the experience was galling: "I've had a lot of pain in my life over what might seem to some [to be] very small things."

Still, it is more than the personal sense of rejection that bothers her; Allen sees in the Harvard ordeal portents of a larger and disturbing trend. In the *Berkeley Women's Law Journal* article, she wrote: "Even successful black women students have felt out of place within higher education. And in the post–civil rights era, black women educators have been made to feel unwelcome. Long before the media caught wind of the controversy over hiring women of color, black women knew that many on campus privately raised the question I was once asked publicly: 'What gives *you* the right to teach this class?'" Among the other lessons Allen has learned is "the fact that including black women in higher education arouses inherent suspicion."

The Management Consultant

Lennox Joseph is executive director and chief executive officer of NTL (National Training Laboratories) Institute, an Alexandria, Virginia–based firm that specializes in workshops, conferences, and other activities aimed at making executives into better managers. He has a Ph.D. in organizational behavior and analysis from Case Western Reserve University and is a respected member of the applied social sciences community. Yet he is troubled. "I have had hell to pay for where I am today," says Joseph, whose melodious voice retains more than a trace of his native Trinidad.

Joseph came to Alexandria by way of Cleveland, where he worked in governmental social programs and was later head of a management consulting group. He left because "I couldn't stand the racism." Joseph recalls going to a nightclub in 1988, a few months before deciding to relocate. Several whites had entered the club before him, but he and a black physician friend were politely rebuffed: "All of a sudden, the club had become 'private.' " A few weeks later, at another club, a black friend who was supposed to meet him inside was turned away at the door. Angry and frustrated, Joseph began to think about moving to a city where his personal comfort level might be higher. Atlanta, Philadelphia, and the D.C. area all seemed to be reasonable alternatives, so he began a job search and accepted the position of director of operations of NTL.

He did well enough that he was soon asked to take the organization's top job, but he was unsure what to make of the offer. For one thing, the title was being changed from president to executive director—almost as if the board intended to signal that "president" was a bit much for Joseph to carry. Not that he didn't have his own doubts about how effectively he could function as NTL's leader. Though he had wealth of professional credentials, he was young—in his mid-thirties—and somewhat unproven. Moreover, he would be the first black person to hold the position, and the board seemed less than totally supportive. "No one was saying, 'Come on Lennox, you'll be great.' " Instead, at least on the part of a few board members, he sensed an attitude that he should be grateful for whatever salary and compensation package they decided to give him. He also sensed resistance from a few people on staff. The woman in charge of marketing, for instance, could never seem to find time to put together a press release announcing his promotion.

Whether or to what extent such resistance was racial was impossible to tell with any precision. But Joseph felt a need, more intense than many white executives might have felt, to build support for himself within NTL. Upon being made executive director, he threw himself into an almost constant round of dinners and meetings with the huge cadre of consultants through which NTL did much of its work. In addition, he held a series of management retreats where an expert in group dynamics encouraged the consultants to explore their feelings about the new boss. At one retreat, at the expert's urging, a consultant drew a picture of how he saw Joseph in relation to himself, showing Joseph as a child being physically supported by the consultant. Joseph found the image indicative of a depressing lack of confidence. It told him that despite his academic accomplishments and international reputation, he was not being taken seriously.

His response was to work even harder at proving himself and winning acceptance. In one five-month period, he took only two weekends off, working virtually around the clock. He appeared in the office at 6:00 A.M. and did not leave until well after dark. The strain of maintaining that schedule left him on the verge of collapse. His social life had vanished, he was putting on weight, and he felt emotionally exhausted. After he suffered a serious blood clot, his physician hospitalized him for a week.

The experience was sobering and made him face up to the effects of the stress he was inflicting on himself. It helped him resolve not only to take better care of himself, but to put his life and its pressures in perspective. Certain burdens, he recognized, would inevitably fall on people like himself—pioneers in areas where few members of the race had gone before. During difficult times, he would remind himself that he and others like him had a special mission, that "part of our role is to create space for other black people to follow us." And despite the stress he would draw a measure of peace from the knowledge that he was "helping to move the race forward."

chapter two *Tiptoeing Around the Truth*

♦♦♦♦♦♦♦♦♦♦♦♦♦♦♦♦♦♦♦♦♦♦♦♦♦♦♦♦♦♦♦♦

$\boxed{D}$URING THE SUMMER OF 1991, I FOUND MYSELF in the presence of Robert Maxwell, the flamboyant and famously eccentric hulk of a British press lord. This was months prior to his death and subsequent revelations that he had looted his own companies; Maxwell, who had recently bought the money-hemorrhaging New York *Daily News*, was widely viewed not as a crook but as the paper's savior.

I was being recruited to come to the *News* as head of its editorial pages and chairman of its editorial board. As part of the process, orchestrated by editor James Willse, I was ushered into Maxwell's $4,000-a-day suite in the Waldorf-Astoria. Along with assorted senior executives seeking approval for various projects, Willse and I waited to be summoned. Eventually, we were shown into a makeshift office where the magisterial Maxwell sat behind a desk. He greeted us and then ignored me for several minutes as he interrogated Willse regarding my credentials and future responsibilities. Apparently satisfied, he signaled Willse to leave and began to pepper me with questions, most having to do with my background and my impressions of the *News*.

Suddenly he shifted focus. What statement would the *News* be making, he asked, by appointing me to the job? I knew where he wanted me to go, but I refused to bite. "You would be saying that you want a top-flight journalist running your editorial pages," I replied. He nodded but clearly judged the answer incomplete. Would the appointment make me, he wanted to know, the top-ranking black newspaperman in New York? I shrugged, saying it all depended on what one made of titles; maybe yes, maybe no. He indicated he was not quite satisfied, and posed the same question in a slightly different fashion. Again I gave an inconclusive answer, having decided—largely out of irritation—that if he wanted to make racial symbolism the center of the conversation he would have to do so on his own. Instead, Maxwell changed the subject, and shortly thereafter, with an imperial wave of the hand, abruptly ended the session.

Obviously, the very fact that I was offered the job meant that in this case my race had not worked against me. If anything, it had worked to my advantage. Certainly, it had not been immaterial.

For most blacks in America, regardless of status, political persuasion, or accomplishments, the moment never arrives when race can be treated as a total irrelevancy. Instead, too often it is the only relevant factor defining our existence.

"A white man with a million dollars is a millionaire, and a black man with a million dollars is a nigger with a million dollars," New York's mayor, David Dinkins, told me over lunch in October 1992, attributing the aphorism to his friend Percy Sutton, the former Manhattan borough president. Dinkins quickly added that he wasn't sure Sutton was the source, and also made clear that the view expressed was not necessarily his own. Yet I suspected the statement captured a sentiment—and a resentment—that burned brightly in Dinkins's heart.

Only two weeks earlier several thousand members of his own police department had staged a raucous anti-Dinkins rally on City Hall's steps. In the course of the demonstration, a few of the cops had flaunted signs: "Dinkins, we know your true color—yellow-bellied," "Dump the Washroom Attendant," "No Justice, No Police." Jimmy Breslin, a *Newsday* columnist on the scene, reported that some of the protesters had shouted, "Now you got a nigger right inside City Hall. How do you like that? A nigger mayor."

Though I had not come to ask Dinkins about the police protest, I knew it weighed heavily on his mind. I also knew that as New York's first black mayor, he had been burdened with more than his share of symbolism. At a time when racial incidents (from verbal assaults to riots to beatings with baseball bats and clubs) exploded upon the city with sickening regularity, Dinkins was expected to be a racial healer—especially by whites, who had denied him a majority of their votes. At the same time, whites, as well as New York's menagerie of minorities, viewed virtually every Dinkins deed through a narrow racial prism.

Yet he was expected not to complain—and not to be bothered by the fact that many regarded him not as the mayor but as the *black mayor*. That very day, I had received a letter from a *Daily News* reader, which she had also sent to Dinkins. She doubted the mayor would read it, so requested that it be printed in the *News*. "It seems you are so concerned, because a police officer used the word 'nigger,' during their demonstration. . . . Why is it always racism when a black person is called nigger, but not when a white person is called a white bitch?" she wrote.

The woman's point seemed to be that Dinkins had no business being upset about being called a nigger, at least not as long as certain blacks felt free to call a white woman a bitch. Essentially she was holding Dinkins responsible for the behavior of those blacks, in a way she probably would never have considered holding a white mayor responsible. But she was also saying something more: that whatever reactions he might have to racism were inconsequential, certainly nothing she wanted to hear. And she was not alone.

"I have gone to great lengths to avoid any complaints about my personal circumstances as respects race," Dinkins confessed at one point. "Many is the reporter who has said to me, 'Do you think you're treated differently because you're black?' . . . And I leave it [to them to] . . . make the observation. 'Why do *you* think this happens or that happens?' " It was pointless to protest, or even to discuss the issues, because "there are people who want to seize upon such things" and accuse him of "playing the race card," or of introducing race to cover up his own alleged inadequacies. Instead of griping about how critics treat him, said Dinkins, "I've complained about how people treat the city. But I've never said it's because I'm black that you're treating me differently than you've treated this one, or would treat another."

He paused briefly and said, almost under his breath, "When I write my memoirs or something, I might be inclined to discuss it more fully. It's not in my interest to talk about my personal circumstances in that regard at this time. . . . I make no complaints." For an instant I thought he had exhausted the subject, but he went on, noting again that when reporters, especially white reporters, pressed him on the question, he made a practice of turning the tables and asking them why they had asked. If they thought he was being treated differently because of race, he wanted to know why the hell they didn't write that instead of trying to put him on the spot. And if they didn't have the courage to write the truth about their own observations, he certainly was not going to take the bait. "Nobody's going to acknowledge it. Nobody's going to admit it. If they think that [a black mayor is subjected to a double standard], they're not going to say it, unless they can tie it to somebody."

Never having asked the mayor whether he thought he was held to an unfair standard, I felt no need to defend those journalists who did. But I was fascinated by the agitation in his voice. Clearly, he was convinced that many people could not see beyond the color of his skin. And clearly he was right. The idea of cops, even enraged white cops, referring to a white mayor as a bathroom attendant, for instance, was absurd. Yet what he felt—and what in fact was true—was not something he permitted himself to say, certainly not on the record. For to speak frankly and honestly about race would be to anger (or perhaps "disaffiliate") those whites who preferred to believe that racism, by and large, had disappeared.

Asked whether it was possible to be honest about race, given that reality, Dinkins replied, "I think it's essential that you be honest about it—*to a degree.*" Certain things, he indicated, were none of the public's business; and he compared his refusal to discuss a possible double standard to his refusal to discuss the frequency of sex with his wife. To me, the comparison made absolutely no sense; while sex is a private affair, a mayor's relationship with the press and public is nothing of the sort. Still, I thought his reading of the degree of candor the public was willing to accept was essentially correct; for when race enters the discussion, more often than not truth slips away.

A few weeks before the conversation with Dinkins, I spent an evening with Basil Paterson, a Dinkins intimate who had served as a deputy mayor in the early part of Ed Koch's administration, was a former vice chair of the Democratic National Committee, and had been the 1970 Democratic candidate for lieutenant governor of New York. As a trailblazing black politician, Paterson had spent plenty of time pondering the art of survival in a predominantly white political system. He had concluded, he said, that "whites don't want you to be angry." So black politicians, in order to get along, often conceal their true feelings. "We're selective in our terminology. We waste a lot of time that ought to be devoted to candor."

Paterson's observation is clearly not true of all black politicians, or even of all those whose constituents are largely white. Some black officeholders behave in just the opposite manner, angrily blaming any misfortune—including being caught in illegal or immoral acts—on bigotry and racist conspiracies. Still, Paterson's words haunted me, for over and over, as I interviewed successful black people from various walks of life, I encountered very similar reactions. Many of these normally outspoken professionals were extremely reluctant to own up to or have attributed to them the anger they clearly felt. To acknowledge their race-related anger or frustration, they feared, would be to alienate (and perhaps provoke reprisals from) those whites whose goodwill was essential to their well-being.

One man, a ranking editor at a major newspaper, revealed that in the wake of the 1992 Los Angeles riots, he had thought of writing an article for his newspaper's magazine about anger among middle-class blacks. He had mentioned the idea to a colleague, who had advised him not to propose it. Even though the colleague thought the topic to be of critical importance, he also felt that writing about it would be dangerous to his friend's career. It would risk rousing the suspicions of powerful white editors who would conclude that he, the writer, was the one who was angry. And it was only a small step from being seen as an angry black man to being labeled a troublemaker. The writer decided to heed the advice, concluding that publishing an important article was hardly worth paying that price.

During an interview, a socially prominent partner in a major law firm passionately denounced racism and noted that many young minority lawyers bitterly complained of its effects, but he equivocated when asked whether it had affected him personally, preferring to keep his public anger focused on a generic grievance. At one point, the conversation turned to prestigious private clubs. He acknowledged that blacks were usually not welcome but added, "You just don't go to places that are not likely to admit you." As for himself, he said he took his pleasures where he could. While he certainly enjoyed his membership in the university-affiliated club that his status as an alumnus allowed him to join, he was not all that eager to join other clubs. Realizing that the answer was transparently disingenuous, he asked if he could say something not for attribution.

There were beautiful tennis courts in a private club a few minutes' walk from his suburban home, and though his white neighbors all belonged, he had never been asked to join. "That annoys me enormously," he admitted as indignation tightened his face. Then he relaxed and quickly added, as if to soften the statement, "We don't care much for those people, anyway."

The reluctance of many members of the black middle class to talk about their anger out loud should not be confused with complacency. It is best understood as a painful adaptation to a society that does not want to hear that privileged members of a generally "underprivileged" group still harbor serious complaints. The problem with such silence is obvious. In the words of Edward Jones, the management consultant, "How the heck do we solve something we can't talk about?" Yet even he concedes that the truth "makes people uncomfortable."

Alvin Poussaint, associate professor of psychiatry at Harvard Medical School and a close advisor to Bill Cosby, sees black self-censorship as a simple tool of survival. "It's always a risk for a black person in a predominantly white corporation to express individual anger," he says, because whites tend not to understand what the anger is about. As a result they are likely to dismiss the complainer as a chronic malcontent or a maladjusted person who perhaps needs to be eased out.

The inability to talk about race in anything resembling honest terms compounds the very misunderstanding that renders silence necessary. For those blacks and whites who come into closest contact, it stands as a huge barrier to their ever truly accepting one another or finding common ground.

Senator Moynihan believes Americans are in "kind of a denial of ethnicity." When he and Nathan Glazer wrote *Beyond the Melting Pot*, people were outraged at their examination of ethnic strife: "By and large the attitude was that 'if you want to talk about this stuff, you encourage it.' " Yet when I remarked on the dissatisfaction rampant within the black middle class, Moynihan dismissed it as essentially groundless. This "upper group" of blacks, he said, was "moving along very well" even though some remained "caught with the legacy of grievance which is inappropriate to their condition." "Those blacks with the jobs are perfectly capable of saying they're being persecuted," he added.

In mentioning Moynihan's observation to several solidly middle-class blacks, I found not one who accepted his pronouncement—even among those who said they had no complaints about their own treatment or situation.

Donald McHenry, former ambassador to the United Nations (a post once held by Moynihan), said: "I don't agree that people are out of sync, if you will, with the level of their progress. One doesn't know how much further you could be along, how many other opportunities would be there." Indeed, many successful blacks know that if it were not for discrimination, they would have done much better. They know because they see others with no greater ability progress far beyond them; and they know that race is all that distinguishes them from their more successful white colleagues. "I think that even people who are in the middle class, or who are higher, still carry with them this resentment, this feeling that somehow they would be further along. How much further along would *I* be, I don't know. The difference between me and most is that I don't let it bother me."

Ron Brown, a psychologist whose San Francisco–based firm, Banks and Brown Inc., specializes in helping corporations manage and motivate multiethnic workforces, took a similar view. Time after time, he has encountered blacks who felt undermined in their work, or who watched less competent whites pass them by. And while they suspected race may have played a role, they could never be sure, partly because the corporations refuse to acknowledge any such possibility. "There is a denial [by the corporation] of any racial factors, when your whole organizational experience tells you there are all kinds of racial factors. . . . So in most cases a lot of people don't even bring it up. . . . It doesn't ever get talked about." And eventually many black executives, once so motivated and raring to go, simply "shut down" in frustration. "If businesses knew that they were somehow coopting and suppressing and stifling thirty to forty percent of their brains, they might say, 'Well, we got to do something. Boy, you're walking around here with only one eye and half a brain working.' But they don't see it that way."

A senior partner in a major Washington law firm was even more emphatic: "Our rage is not basically just directed at [conditions in the workplace]," he said. "It's not just money. It's not just my house." It has to do with being totally and capriciously stripped of status at a moment's notice. It has to do, he said, with going into a store "where there's a white redneck who treats me like I make two cents and am uneducated," despite his degrees and high-powered job. "What needs to happen to Moynihan," he railed, is for him to wake up one day in an America that has decided, " 'We're going to kick the shit out of them [Irish-Americans] on every level except their salary and their job. You come to work, etcetera; but every other part of your life we're going to kick the shit out of you.' And then you may understand how it feels."

William Raspberry, a *Washington Post* columnist, told me: "African Americans are not yet at the point where we can react in political and social terms entirely as individuals. White people can pretty much react as individuals." If whites are not doing as well as they had hoped, said Raspberry, they can chalk it up to either bad luck or some personal failing, whereas blacks are much more likely to conclude that "a major part of . . . not doing well" relates to the color of their skin. "And we don't dare become comfortable with our own situation as long as skin color still plays a major role in the prospects of people who look like us."

"People don't stop being angry just because they get money or get position," said Alvin Poussaint, the psychiatrist from Harvard, not as long as they face an unending stream of psychological slights. He knows black doctors who dress up to go shopping, simply to avoid being taken for shoplifters; and he knows major celebrities who feel excluded from the white old-boy Hollywood network where deals get made. "If you're black and middle-class . . . every day you're [going to get] a lot of crap. You're going to get angry."

Certainly, examples of angry celebrated blacks are easy to find. Filmmaker Spike Lee has become notorious for his vehement harangues against racism. But even among those who shy away from the role of black spokesperson and whose persona is anything but contentious or hostile, a sense of racial estrangement is palpable. Michael Morgan, the acclaimed classical conductor, told a writer for the *New York Times* in 1992: "I have a very nice little career now, but I also know that sometimes that's because it has been to the advantage of an organization to have me, an African American, around. I see what others my age do, and that there are more star-studded careers that I have no doubt I would have if I were not black."

The people I interviewed about Moynihan's observation were obviously not a scientifically selected sample. It's possible they represent a fringe perspective or are all in the state of denial that Moynihan describes. I suspect, however, that something more is at work, that even if the depth of grievance is "inappropriate to their condition," the sense of injustice is not unfounded; and the plight is compounded by a society that in large measure insists that middle-class blacks have nothing to complain about.

Among successful blacks—and among many who belong to other ethnic minority groups as well—the number who spend much of their energy fighting desperation is alarmingly high, notwithstanding that we live in an age where legions of white men have concluded *they* are the group most discriminated against. That the pain of those blacks is generally invisible to whites in part reflects the fact that voicing it can carry consequences. Neither bosses nor colleagues much care for a crybaby—especially when they cannot understand what lies behind the tears.

In contrast, America easily understands, or thinks it does, the raw racial rage of the ghetto. Prose portraits of the nation's bullet-ridden slums have permitted even the most sequestered suburban-ites to view an inner-city hell of drugs, squalid housing, and low expectations, where alienation thrives. When explosions come—as in South Central Los Angeles in 1992 or Miami's Liberty City in 1980 and 1989—the cause is presumed to be clear. For those on the left, it lies in the wretchedness of inner-city life, in society's cold destruction of the human spirit. For those on the right, it stems from a poverty of values, from the inability and unwilling-ness of flawed people to take control of their lives and assume responsibility for their destiny. The explanations may be contra-dictory, but somewhere within or between them, most people believe, lies the secret to inner-city rage.

Rage among members of the black middle class is something different altogether. This is not a group that has any right to bellyache or wallow in self-pity—not if that right is won by dint of conspicuous suffering. After all, the economic and social status of many of its members is far higher than the level most Americans of any race have achieved.

At the celebrity super-rich level, the increased prominence of blacks has been impossible to miss. Bill Cosby has become a fixture atop the *Forbes* list of the nation's highest-paid entertain-ers. In 1992, the magazine put the comedian's gross earnings for the most recent two years at $98 million. Talk-show host Oprah Winfrey came in at $88 million, and singers Michael Jackson and Prince at $51 million and $45 million, respectively.

But even well below that stratospheric level, many African Americans are doing quite nicely. According to U.S. Census fig-ures, from 1967 to 1991 the proportion of black households earn-ing $50,000 or more a year (in 1991 dollars) rose from 5.2 to 12.1

percent, or roughly 1.3 million households. The proportion earning $100,000 and up in those same years more than doubled, from .5 percent to 1.2 percent. Though the figures lagged far behind those for white households (27.5 percent with incomes of $50,000 and above in 1991, and 4.8 with incomes of at least $100,000), they obviously meant that the black upper middle class was growing.

In 1978, sociologist William Julius Wilson published an influential and important book, *The Declining Significance of Race*. Many read the title but not the tome and leapt to the conclusion that race no longer mattered in America. In fact, Wilson was saying nothing of the sort. He was making an argument a good deal more subtle, and also a good deal less exact. The "life chances of individual blacks have more to do with their economic class position than with their day-to-day encounters with whites," he concluded, citing a wealth of evidence that more blacks than ever were moving into white-collar jobs and skilled craft and foremen positions. He had little to say, however, about what happened once they got into those jobs, whether they moved up the ladder, or whether these privileged individuals ever managed to achieve their full potential.

The examination of such matters was not Wilson's purpose. His real concern was the black underclass, and the major point he set out to make was that the problems of that class could not be attributed to race alone, but were largely the consequence of certain economic developments. He was so disturbed that his short section on the black middle class received such disproportionate attention that he later published another book, *The Truly Disadvantaged*, which explicitly focused on the urban underclass. In it, he lambasted reviewers for their fixation on the middle-class section of his previous book: it "seemed that critics were so preoccupied with what I had to say about the improving condition of the black middle class that they virtually ignored my more important arguments about the deteriorating conditions of the black underclass."

The response to Wilson's remarks about the black middle class is hardly remarkable. America likes success stories. We also prefer to believe that our country—give or take a David Duke or two—is well on the road to being color-blind. And since the predicament of the black underclass seems so hopeless, many find it comforting to concentrate on those who are doing well. Moreover, it is the black middle class, with its solid values and material attributes of success, that many deep thinkers have concluded may be the salvation of the down and out.

In a provocative 1988 article in *Esquire* magazine, Pete Hamill lamented that there was "very little now that whites can do in a direct way for the maimed and hurting citizens of the Underclass." The way to the light, he argued, would have to be cleared by blacks who had made it into the middle class. "I've come to believe that if there is to be a solution to the self-perpetuating Underclass, it must come from blacks, specifically from the black middle class. Blacks might have no other choice."

More recently political scientist James Q. Wilson has made a similar argument. "The best way to reduce racism real or imagined is to reduce the black crime rate," he says. "Decent black people" must assume major responsibility for transforming the lives of black infants so that crime rates will plummet. Those solidly responsible blacks "must accept, and ideally should develop and run, whatever is done."

The irony in such arguments is that the "decent black people" who will save America from the underclass, those paragons of middle-class virtue who will rescue the ghetto from violence, are themselves in a state of either silent resentment or deeply repressed rage. Taken as a group, they are at least as disaffected and pessimistic as those struggling at society's periphery. They consistently report more encounters with racial prejudice and voice stronger reservations about the country's success at delivering on the American dream. In a 1991 *Los Angeles Times* poll 58 percent of "affluent" blacks and 54 percent of college-educated blacks reported experiencing job- or education-related prejudice—higher numbers than were recorded for those who were poor and had no college education.

A May 1991 survey by the Gallup Organization asked, "Looking back over the last ten years, do you think the quality of life of blacks has gotten better, stayed about the same, or gotten worse?" Seventy percent of blacks with a college education felt things had gotten worse. Only 55 percent of those without a college education felt that way. Conversely, only 8 percent of the college-educated thought things had gotten better, compared to 18 percent of those without college.

In 1990, the Gallup Organization conducted a poll for *Newsday* in Long Island—its first ever of well-to-do suburban blacks—and discovered that two-thirds of those interviewed complained of discrimination. Three-fourths were convinced that realtors in the area steered blacks away from white neighborhoods. Respondents were significantly less satisfied with their lives than whites with substantially lower incomes. "Diane Colasanto, the Gallup vice president who prepared *Newsday*'s poll, said that because blacks are better off on Long Island than in most other areas she had expected that they would have more positive views," reported the paper.

When I spoke with Colasanto in 1992, she said she had not been surprised at the results at all because some of her earlier work had also revealed "these feelings of separateness" among middle-class blacks. She had meant to communicate to *Newsday* her sense that the results were important, that they merited serious attention in part because they were so at odds with society's expectations.

Why would people who have enjoyed all the fruits of the civil rights revolution—who have Ivy League educations, high-paying jobs, and comfortable homes—be quietly seething inside? To answer that question is to go a long way toward explaining why quotas and affirmative action remain such polarizing issues; why black and white Americans continue to see race in such starkly different terms; and why solving America's racial problems is infinitely more complicated than cleaning up the nation's urban ghettos and educating the inhabitants—even assuming the will, wisdom, and resources to accomplish such a task.

Statistics tell only part of the story—though the part they tell is revealing. An analysis by Queens College of the City University of New York, for instance, shows that despite huge shifts in New York City's population, blacks and whites—regardless of income—remain as segregated now as ten years ago, and that for blacks race is a far more accurate indicator of where they are likely to live than economic class. Research by the Urban Institute indicates that in America's fifty largest metropolitan areas, 37 percent of blacks live in segregated neighborhoods, and that blacks experience discrimination 53 percent of the times they try to rent a home, and 59 percent of the times they look to buy one.

The inner sanctum of the corporate world remains largely segregated. Though the number of blacks earning high incomes has risen, only a handful have climbed near the top of the corporate structure. In 1989, Korn Ferry International replicated a 1979 survey of senior executives in Fortune 500 firms. In that ten-year interval, blacks went from .2 percent to .6 percent, and all minorities (blacks, Hispanics, and Asians) went from .5 percent to 1.3 percent.

In the real world such statistics are almost irrelevant, for rage does not flow from dry numerical analyses of discrimination or from professional prospects projected on a statistician's screen. It flows from the felt experiences of everyday life, from lessons learned in run-of-the-mill human encounters, from the struggles and disappointments of family members and peers. It comes from learning that one can never take the kindness—or the acceptance—of strangers for granted; from resentment at being judged at every turn, if only in part, for one's complexion instead of oneself.

Bill Bradley, U.S. senator from New Jersey, speaks of his career as a professional basketball player as "those ten years I lived in a sort of a black world." As a result, Bradley told me, "I did see . . . things I would not have seen, and felt things that I would not have felt, had I not been in that group at that time on the road in America." For instance, he learned what it means never to be able to relax, never to know where the next insult or slight would come from. "And that is what's so depressing about it. You can't just [say], 'Well that's settled.' You want to get to a point [where you can drop your guard]." But that point, he indicated, never seemed to come.

What that means in the context of daily experience is being

forced to bear what Isabel Wilkerson, Chicago bureau chief for the *New York Times*, calls "the incredible burden of living this dual life . . . and being constantly reduced to third-class citizenship and still expected to operate . . . with a smile on your face after one thing after another."

Asked for specific incidents, Wilkerson let go with a virtual catalog. Once, upon arriving at the airport in Detroit, she found that she was running late for an interview. She raced through the terminal and was about to hop aboard an Avis bus when a man and a woman, both white, ran up behind her, announced they were with the Drug Enforcement Administration, and demanded that she step aside. She told them she couldn't afford to miss the bus, so they climbed on with her and watched her every move. Initially, she was "astonished and in kind of a daze" as it sunk in that she was suspected of carrying drugs. She was not too dazed to notice, however, that she was the only black person on the bus. As the agents stared at her, she found herself growing both angry and intensely embarrassed. "There was absolutely no reason for them to stop me except [that] I was black." When they tried to interrogate her, she took out her note pad and "ended up trying to do a little reverse psychology." She started asking them questions, mostly to help her keep her presence of mind. Still, as she realized the entire bus was staring, humiliation washed over her, and she wondered whether rape could be much worse. She was eventually let go without having to submit to a search, but she nonetheless found the experience "wrenching."

In another instance Wilkerson had to endure an interrogation from a secretary concerning her educational and professional credentials before being allowed to speak to an executive she was scheduled to interview. Though she was Chicago bureau chief, she had quickly learned not to trot out the title, since so many people refused to believe that she could possess the professional standing she claimed. Such things reminded her, said Wilkerson, that her status as a middle-class person was provisional, that "being a part of the middle-class professional society's world" was in many respects an "illusion."

This sense of the permanent vulnerability of one's status surfaced repeatedly in the interviews I conducted. Lynn Walker, a Ford Foundation executive, related how the residents of her co-op once resolved to determine which apartment dweller was misguidedly mixing construction debris in with the trash. Along with her white neighbors, she was picking through the garbage outside her building one morning, searching for evidence of ownership, when a white homeless person chanced upon the group of foragers. He paused, then walked directly up to Walker and helpfully advised her that he had already scoured the rubbish and found nothing worthwhile. For a moment she was confused, but she suddenly realized that though she was dressed for work, the man had taken her for a fellow homeless person. Later she laughed over the bizarre episode but observed that it had driven home for her how pervasive a role racial assumptions can play.

Knowing that race can undermine status, African Americans frequently take aggressive countermeasures in order to avoid embarrassment. One woman, a Harvard-educated lawyer, learned to carry a Bally bag when going to certain exclusive shops. Like a sorceress warding off evil with a wand, she would hold the bag in front of her to rebuff racial assumptions, in the hope that the clerk would take it as proof that she could be trusted to enter. A prominent sociologist with a national reputation confessed to a similar frustration. The saleswoman at a shop on New York's East Side refused to budge until his white girlfriend, who was already inside, asked, "Why aren't you letting him in?" When the woman finally opened the door, the sociologist was so enraged that he told her off and left.

My own wife, Lee, who is Puerto Rican, went apartment hunting by herself when we were considering moving. In one building after another, she got the distinct impression that she was being condescended to. A superintendent took one look at her and slammed the door, telling her not to disturb him while he was eating. When she called a listing and asked the pleasant-sounding woman on the other end whether the apartment (advertised without an address) was in a good neighborhood, the woman responded, "Yes, it's a very good neighborhood. There are no black people here." On another occasion, she went to see a broker who insisted—despite our high income and Fifth Avenue address—on showing her one slum apartment after another. Only after she impressed on the woman that she was a lawyer and a prosecutor was she taken to a decent place—a studio so much smaller than the two- or three-bedroom apartment we had requested that the agent knew there was no possibility we would take it. Finally, in frustration, Lee gave up her search for the day. Later, her voice trembling with outrage, she declared, "Next time I go looking for an apartment, I'm taking somebody white along with me."

The pain and anger inflicted by such experiences do not quickly go away. Conrad K. Harper, a partner in the New York law firm Simpson Thacher & Barlett, recalls with precision the time, more than a decade and half ago, when a broker called to tell him the deal had collapsed for a Westchester home he had planned to buy. He asked whether race was a factor and to his astonishment the broker confessed that it was. Harper sued, the broker testified in his behalf, and he eventually got his home. Yet despite the passage of time, says Harper, the experience "still makes me angry. At some level that particularly grates."

Reminders that one's humanity is automatically devalued because of race come in many forms—including what journalist Joseph Boyce calls the "black tax." A former Atlanta bureau chief of *Time* magazine, Boyce tells the story of his 1985 move to New York, where he was to become deputy bureau chief. Because Time Inc. had a policy of buying transferred employees' current homes at 105 percent of appraised value, it was in his interest to get a high appraisal. The first appraisal on his four-bedroom house came in significantly lower than expected, and Boyce, who is black, wondered whether his race was blinding the realtors to its true value, so he summoned another team of realtors. On the appointed day, he moved out and had his white secretary move in. She replaced the photographs of his beaming family with hers, and when the appraiser arrived she waltzed around the house as if she had lived there all her life. The result was an appraised value nearly 15 percent above the prior assessment. Though Boyce, now a senior editor at the *Wall Street Journal*, tells the tale with genuine humor, it is laced with weary resignation—a resignation born of the recognition that had he been a whit less clever his color, quite literally, would have cost him. And indeed still could.

As a consequence of the need for such constant alertness, even the most mild-mannered individuals sometimes find themselves boiling over with anger. Yet James Baldwin had it wrong. To be black and "relatively conscious" in America is not necessarily to be in a perpetual state of rage. Few human beings of any race could survive the psychic toll of uninterrupted anger. Those who did would be in such a miserable state that they could scarcely cope with life, much less succeed at it. In successful individuals, especially those who are members of racial minority groups, even righteous rage tends to be leavened with humor and grace. What is constant is not anger but awareness, awareness that even the most pleasant interracial encounter can suddenly become awkward, ugly, or worse.

In 1986, management consultant Edward Jones published an article in the *Harvard Business Review* reporting on his three-year research project on blacks in corporate America. Jones interviewed more than two hundred corporate managers and designed two surveys of blacks with MBA degrees, both too small and too casually conducted to stand up to serious scientific scrutiny. One, for instance, consisted of mailing a twenty-three-page questionnaire to 305 graduates of the nation's top five business schools, from whom he received 107 completed replies. Still, the findings were revealing: among that small group sampled by Jones, the degree of discontent was staggering. Nearly all respondents claimed that black managers did not enjoy equal opportunity at their firms. Ninety-eight percent said that subtle prejudice pervaded their companies. Ninety percent reported a "climate of support" worse than that for their white peers. Eighty-four percent said that race had worked to their disadvantage when it came to ratings, pay, assignments, recognition, performance appraisals, and promotion. Fewer than 10 percent reported a work atmosphere that encouraged open discussion of racial issues.

"It doesn't matter whether, by some impossible objective standard, these people are right or wrong; what counts is how they feel," Jones concluded. Interestingly, what they felt directly contradicted the view of the overwhelming majority of white senior executives who assured Jones that their corporations were "color-blind."

When I spoke to Jones in 1992, he was no longer conducting surveys. He had continued doing them for several years after his original research came out, but "I stopped . . . because I wasn't finding anything different than in the '86 survey." From his ongoing work with black managers, however, Jones suspected that the situation might even be worse. "Some of us are losing hope. The psychological casualty rate is very high." Anyone who had spent much time in honest contact with black professionals would not have been surprised at his survey results—or at his melancholic supposition.

Shortly before Jones's *Harvard Business Review* article appeared, I found myself working closely with an array of young managers who in many respects resembled those whose feelings he so poignantly delineated. As one of my responsibilities as head of a nonprofit journalism training institution headquartered in Berkeley, California, I spent most of a summer at Northwestern University in Evanston, Illinois, running an eight-week executive program. I had designed the seminar in conjunction with a task force of newspaper executives from across the country, along with faculty from Northwestern's graduate schools of business and journalism. Its purpose was to train a multiethnic cadre of newspaper managers, individuals who had been identified by their organizations as likely to become leaders in their companies and in their field. Though some members of the class were white, most were black or belonged to various other minority groups. Not only were they to be immersed in such technical subjects as accounting, marketing, and financial management, but they also were to be provided time and opportunity to grapple with racial and gender questions that business schools typically ignore. Such questions as: Do minority and white managers face fundamentally different tasks? How low and how real is the glass ceiling? Can one get beyond (and help others get beyond) prejudice and preconceptions?

One evening I scheduled a session led by Ron Brown, the psychologist and specialist in interracial relations, who has an awesome ability to cut straight through to people's emotional core. Part inspirational speaker, part father-confessor, Brown impatiently paced the floor, tossing off anecdotes and pointed questions, challenging his listeners to shed their professional reserve. Precisely as he had known would happen, anger, confusion, and pain came pouring out. How could they cope with bosses who judged them by a different standard than whites? With coworkers who resented their presence? With constantly having to prove that despite their color, they were still part of the team? Was it possible, one woman asked, to hold on to her black identity and be a success in the white corporate world? Was it realistic, another asked, to expect to be treated as anything other than a well-paid, poorly-utilized token?

Earlier in the day, a high-ranking lawyer in a major corporation had presented a short tutorial. Though he was attending the session as a guest, he was so affected by the dynamics in the room that he felt compelled to open up. He told of his surprise a few months ago at being invited to his chief executive officer's home for the weekend. Never before had such an invitation been extended—at least in part, he assumed, because his boss simply didn't socialize with blacks. So he panicked, concluding that something dramatic and hugely important must be afoot. He spent days dreading the weekend, worrying about just what that something might be, but when he finally arrived at the man's home, he discovered that all his worries had been for naught. His boss simply wanted to get to know him better. If he had been white, the lawyer thought, he would have assumed that from the beginning. Being black, he was accustomed to being excluded. He was accustomed, in short, to being treated less as a professional than as a *black* professional.

As anecdotes and questions careened around the room, I was mesmerized—not because the ordeals related were surprising or the group's anxiety about the future unexpected, but because of the sheer intensity of feeling. It was as if in venting their perceptions and experiences, in discovering that their confusion and anger were shared by others, the class felt free to open the floodgates to a powerful set of emotions they generally kept trapped deep within.

Such emotions do not develop in a vacuum. They arise in response to experiences that many members of racial minority groups share, regardless of achievement or status—experiences preserved as painfully recalled snapshots of moments when racial reality rears and slaps one in the face with stunning rudeness. These moments typically begin long before the age at which one enters the work world, and they accumulate throughout life.

The pain of rejection based on race and the desperate attempts to deal with it are of course not unique to our era. In 1957, the well-known black sociologist E. Franklin Frazier published *Black Bourgeoisie*, a devastating portrait of the black middle class, which Frazier held in contempt. He saw it as a class filled with self-hatred and worshipful of a "white" or light complexion, a group "without cultural roots in either the Negro world with which it refuses to identify, or the white world which refuses to permit the black bourgeoisie to share its life." As a consequence, its members had retreated into a pathetic and pathological dream world of society events, self-important preening, and distorted perceptions, whose major function was to insulate them from reality while rewarding them with the status the white world denied.

While remnants of those attitudes are still around, most of today's black American middle class bears little resemblance to that 1950s caricature. They exist in a world where black aspirations are no longer guaranteed to rouse white hostility, in a country where the promise of equality sometimes seems within their reach. Their primary objective is not to escape into an unreal universe, but simply to get what they feel they deserve.

A few weeks after I began conducting interviews for this book, I found myself in the office of an immensely successful corporate lawyer, not only a senior partner in one of the nation's premier law firms, but a bona fide rainmaker, one of the biggest generators

of billings for the partnership. Though we were longtime acquaintances, the meeting was not planned. My appointment was not
with him but with a colleague of his. I stopped by his office on a
whim, on the odd chance he might be in. As I entered, he was
sitting behind his desk, apparently absorbed in a mass of papers,
but he bounded up and greeted me warmly, waving off my apology for interrupting.

Under his polite prompting, I briefly summarized my work-in-
progress. I was dealing with rage, I told him, specifically with the
rage of the black middle class, with why so many people who had
so many things to celebrate seemed to be angry. "Well, I can tell
you why I'm angry," he said, launching into a long tale about his
compensation package. Despite the tens of millions he had
brought into the firm the year before, his partners were balking at
giving him his due. "They want you to do well, but not *that* well,"
he grumbled. The more he talked, the more agitated he became.
What I had originally thought would be a five-minute conversation stretched on for nearly an hour as this normally restrained
and unfailingly gracious man vented long-buried feelings.

Much more was on his mind, it quickly became clear, than the
fact that his partners were still "fumbling with my compensation." One source of immense resentment was an encounter of a
few days previous, when he had arrived at the office an hour or so
earlier than usual and entered the elevator along with a young
white man. They got off at the same floor. No secretaries or
receptionists were yet in place. As my friend fished in a pocket for
his key card while turning toward the locked outer office doors,
his elevator mate blocked his way and asked, "May I help you?"
My friend shook his head and attempted to circle around his
would-be helper, but the young man stepped in front of him and
demanded in a loud and decidedly colder tone, "May I help you?"
At this, the older man fixed him with a stare, spat out his name,
and identified himself as a partner, whereupon his inquisitor
quickly stepped aside.

My friend's initial impulse was to put the incident behind him,
to write it off as merely another annoyance in an ordinary day. Yet
he had found himself growing angrier and angrier at the young

associate's temerity, and his anger returned as he related the event. After all, he had been dressed much better than the associate. His clients paid the younger man's salary. The only thing that could have conceivably given the associate pause was race: "Because of his color, he felt he had the right to check me out."

He paused in his narration and shook his head. "Here I am, a black man who has done all the things I was supposed to do," he said, and proceeded to tick off precisely what he done: gone to Harvard, labored for years to make his mark in an elite law firm, married a highly motivated woman who herself had an advanced degree and a lucrative career. He and his wife were in the process of raising three exemplary children. He had surmounted every hurdle life had thrown in his way. Yet he was far from fulfilled.

"Blacks who have made it up the ladder have had to put up with a lot more crap" than have those who had given up along the way. But these successful people, he mused, were the very ones likely to be especially sensitive to the "crap" they encountered. For if they were not hypersensitive to unspoken racial messages, they would never have been able to avoid society's traps, they would never have gotten as far as they had. He was convinced, however, that the disaffection he felt was not merely a reflection of heightened sensitivity. The world, from his vantage point, was in fact very unfair. "You do have to work harder, every step of the way, and you have got more obstacles than a white person." White people, he added, did not have put up with such affronts as he had experienced at the hands of the young white associate. He was not at all sure what whites who didn't know him personally saw when they encountered him, he said. "I think they see a dark blur, and to them that is inferiority."

I tried to turn the discussion to his obvious success, to the fact that whatever insults he may have felt, he was doing extremely well. He nodded in acknowledgment and responded with words whose essence I would hear repeatedly during my interviews: "Had I been given a fair shot, who knows where I would be?"

Moreover, despite his own clear achievements, he was concerned for his children. With so many black men in jail or beaten down by society, whom would his daughters marry? With prejudice still such a force, who could assure their success? As for himself, he said, he had come to terms with reality. He no longer expected praise, honor, or acceptance from his white colleagues, or from the white world at large. "Just make sure my money is at the top of the line. I can go to my own people for acceptance."

I was certain he did not mean what he said. If acceptance was not important to him, the perceived lack of it would not have caused him such pain. If anything, he was trying to convince himself not to care, trying to make his peace with his certainty that he would never be fully accepted by many of his peers, that even many of his subordinates would consider themselves in some sense his superiors. Because I, in effect, had given him permission, he had let loose a waterfall of anger and frustration that he normally had sense enough to keep locked inside.

When I described the encounter to Ron Brown, he said the man's reaction was totally consistent with what he had seen a thousand times. When the partner had been blocked by the young associate, "it was the momentary and ultimate sign that you're not in. You make $200,000 or more a year. You pay this associate's salary. . . . What you don't get are the same privileges and prerogatives. He feels the privilege to stop you based on nothing else but color. . . . And that [becomes] a symbol [to the senior partner] of times he has gone to a client's office and security guards or secretaries ask, 'Who's this guy?' He's gotten over that. Or times when a client really didn't work with him, really would have preferred to work with a white partner. He's mastered that. All of that mastering and honing, and then where it comes out is right at this point, with this associate. You manage that over a lifetime. You take the slights. And you manage the ability to take the slights. Then, at some point [it all comes tumbling down]."

Brown recalled being in a car with a black general and several other blacks near a military base in Biloxi, Mississippi. As they approached the gates to the base, the general said, "Don't worry," and flashed his two-star badge. The guard replied, "No sir," and demanded to see some identification. "And you could just tell from the back he [the general] was rocking with rage. . . . These little incidents boil over where you should feel ownership," said

Brown. "Where you should feel pride. You should feel privilege. Then some incident comes along . . . right in your domain, to tell you you're not a member. You don't belong here. . . . And everything comes out."

What struck me, however, was not that everything occasionally came tumbling out, but how much was constantly being held in. My experience with that lawyer was far from unique. In encounter after encounter with successful, confident black professionals, I ran into a reservoir of despair so deep that it seemed a blessing (or even a life-sustaining miracle) that their good humor and high spirits had survived.

chapter three *A Dozen Demons*

◆◆◆◆◆◆◆◆◆◆◆◆◆◆◆◆◆◆◆◆◆◆◆◆◆◆◆◆

T HE REVEREND CECIL WILLIAMS IS PERHAPS San Francisco's most famous minister. His Glide Memorial United Methodist Church—for those in the know—has become a tourist attraction more alluring than the Golden Gate Bridge. Celebrities of all races routinely appear in his pews to listen to his forceful message of empowerment and change. Yet though the bearded and ebullient pastor presides over a devoted multiracial congregation, he allows himself few illusions about the irrelevance of race.

One reason may be that for Williams, rejection by whites quite literally drove him mad. In his 1992 book, *No Hiding Place*, Williams writes about growing up in San Angelo, Texas, in the 1930s and '40s. The civil rights movement had not yet been born, and segregation was the established way of life. As a youth, he recalls singing along with his brother for white groups like the Kiwanis club but being ushered out once the performance ended. He remembers being told repeatedly, sometimes subtly and sometimes outright, that neither he nor anyone else in his family would ever be allowed to amount to much. Williams's crisis occurred at the age of ten, when his beloved maternal grandfather, Papa Jack, died. As the funeral procession entered the cemetery, Williams felt a wave of relief. At least, he told himself, Papa Jack would be buried in a peaceful, lovely place with velvety grass and beautiful bouquets. The thought turned to horror when he was informed that they were simply passing through the white section. His grandfather was to be buried in the tract reserved for blacks: an unkempt pasture where, instead of tombstones, plastic-covered notepaper marked the graves of the dead. "Even in death," thought Williams, "Papa Jack and all of us were destined to be nameless and unremembered, while the white folks lay beneath manicured sod and marble memorials."

The death of his grandfather and the grim epiphany in the cemetery precipitated a crippling loss of faith, and Williams plunged into insanity. In the throes of a nervous breakdown, he heard alien voices beckoning him, urging him not to fight his fate, to "accept the life of a nigger in the South" and make his peace with the fact that he would never achieve any standing in relationships with whites. Williams resisted and eventually recovered, but the experience left him shaken.

When he stopped by my office in 1992 as he was traveling through the country to promote his new book, I asked him about the meaning of that episode from childhood. "It's awful," he replied. "I still feel that humiliation [visited upon him by whites] was really the deepest part of that void which disturbed my sanity." But out of that humiliation, he had drawn a certain strength, an attitude, he suspected, very much like that shown by eighteenth-century black poet Phillis Wheatley when she was obliged to audition her poetry before a panel of white men, an attitude of resistance "that says you will not defeat me."

Though Williams has far exceeded any expectations he might reasonably have held as a child growing up in Texas, and done so in a multiracial world, he still feels that he can never fully let his racial guard down; for ghosts from the graveyard in San Angelo, Texas, continue to reappear. "Every once in a while," he said, "when one of my white AIDS patients dies, they go to some other place . . . and they have the memorial." Just the other day, the mother of one such parishioner had made plans to have her son memorialized by a white pastor. That decision, it was clear, had caused Williams pain; and made him feel used: "As long as I can be of service to you, and make things work for you, then you're here. But when it's over, then you go to some other place."

He considered the mother's deed "an act of racism." He smiled, adding, "those things crop up." Even if he personally did not experience prejudice, "I would still know there was a lot of work to be done." He never allowed himself to assume that "I got it made with white folks," because "when the chips are down . . . they're not going to come to me, more than likely."

Daniel Patrick Moynihan may be correct in suggesting that some of the anger felt by successful African Americans stems from a historical sense of racial wrongs, but a major part of Williams's unease is clearly rooted in the here and now. And in that regard he is not alone. The distress Williams experiences when a white family decides to take its memorial service elsewhere is similar to what a black financial manager feels upon being told that a client is uncomfortable with his handling an account, or what a black professor goes through upon being asked whether she is really qualified to teach. Taken separately, such episodes may not amount to much; everyone, regardless of race, experiences occasional slights and even outright rejection. But for many black professionals, these are not so much isolated incidents as insistent and galling reminders that whatever they may accomplish in life, race remains their most salient feature as far as much of America is concerned.

In the workplace, the continuing relevance of race takes on a special force, partly because so much of life, at least for middle-class Americans, is defined by work, and partly because even people who accept that they will not be treated fairly in the world often hold out hope that their work will be treated fairly—that even a society that keeps neighborhoods racially separate and often makes after-hours social relations awkward will properly reward hard labor and competence. What most African Americans discover, however, is that the racial demons that have plagued them all their lives do not recognize business hours—that the stress of coping extends to a nonwork world that is chronically unwilling (or simply unable) to acknowledge the status their professions ought to confer.

The coping effort, in some cases, is relatively minor. It means accepting the fact, for instance, that it is folly to compete for a taxi on a street corner with whites. It means realizing that prudence dictates dressing up whenever you are likely to encounter strangers (including clerks, cops, and doormen) who can make your life miserable by mistaking you for a tramp, a slut, or a crook. And it means tolerating the unctuous boor whose only topic of party conversation is blacks he happens to know. But the price of this continual coping is not insignificant. In addition to creating an unhealthy level of stress, it puts many in such a wary state of mind that insults are seen where none were intended, often complicating communications even with sensitive, well-meaning whites who unwittingly stumble into the racial minefield.

What is it exactly that blacks spend so much time coping with? For lack of a better phrase, let's call them the dozen demons. This is not to say that they affect blacks only; as will become clear, members of other racial minority groups are often plagued by them as well. Nor is it to say that there are only twelve, or that all black Americans encounter every one. Still, if you're looking for a safe bet, you could not find one more certain than this: that any random gathering of black American professionals, asked what irks or troubles them, will eventually end up describing, in one guise or another, the following items.

1 / *Inability to fit in.* During the mid 1980s, I had lunch in the Harvard Club in Manhattan with a newsroom recruiter from the *New York Times*. The lunch was primarily social, but my companion was also seeking help in identifying black, Hispanic, and Asian-American journalists he could lure to the *Times*. Though he had encountered plenty of people with good professional credentials, he was concerned about an attribute that was torturously difficult to gauge: the ability to fit into the often bewildering culture of the *Times*. He was desperate to hire good minority candidates, he said, yet hiring someone who could produce decent copy was not enough. He wanted people with class, people who could be "*Times* people."

As we talked, it became clear that he was focusing on such things as speech, manners, dress, and educational pedigree. He had in mind, apparently, a certain button-down sort, an intellectual, nonthreatening, quiet-spoken type—something of a cross between William F. Buckley and Bill Cosby. Someone who might be expected to have his own membership at the Harvard or Yale

Club. Not surprisingly, he was not having much success. That most whites at the *Times* fit no such stereotype seemed not to have occurred to him. I suggested, rather gingerly, that perhaps he needed to expand his definition of a *"Times* person," that perhaps some of those he was eliminating for seemingly superficial reasons might have all the qualities the *Times* required.

Even as I made the argument, I knew that it was unpersuasive. Not because he disagreed—he did not offer much of a rebuttal—but because he and many similarly placed executives almost instinctively screened minority candidates according to criteria they did not apply to whites. The practice has nothing to do with malice. It stems more, I suspect, from an unexamined assumption that whites, purely because they are white, are likely to fit in, while blacks and other minority group members are not. Hence, he found it necessary to search for specific assurances that those he brought into the fold had qualities that would enable them, despite their color, to blend into the great white mass.

2 / *Exclusion from the club.* Even the ability to fit in, however, does not necessarily guarantee acceptance. Many blacks who have made huge efforts to get the right education, master the right accent, and dress in the proper clothes still find that certain doors never seem to open, that there are private clubs—in both a real and a symbolic sense—they cannot join.

In 1992, a young black corporate lawyer gained considerable notoriety by deflating his résumé and briefly working (while researching an article) as a busboy at an exclusive all-white club. What he found—that some whites, in such an environment, say and do racially obnoxious things—was not earthshaking, or even especially surprising. Nonetheless, his article made the cover of *New York* magazine and set off discussions all over the country, not only about the practice of barring blacks from clubs, but about the larger phenomenon of social acceptance. For whatever other functions these clubs may serve, they do one thing exceptionally well: They tell the world, in the most explicit way, that blacks are not welcome at the top of the social pyramid.

In 1990, in testimony before the U.S. Senate Judiciary Committee, Darwin Davis, senior vice president of the Equitable Life Assurance Society, told of the frustrations he and some of his black friends had experienced in trying to join a country club. "I have openly approached fellow executives about memberships. Several times, they have said, 'My club has openings; it should be no problem. I'll get back to you.' Generally, one of two things happens. They are too embarrassed to talk to me or they come right out and tell me they were shocked when they made inquiries about bringing in a black. Some have even said they were told to get out of the club if they didn't like the situation as it is."

Davis, a white-haired, elegant, and genial raconteur who loves to play golf, told the Senate panel that his interest was not merely in the game but in the financial costs of exclusion. He was routinely reduced to entertaining golf-playing clients at public courses with poor facilities. "The best I can offer my client is a hamburger and a beer in a plastic cup. My competitor takes this client . . . where they have a great lunch and drinks, and use of the locker room and showers. Then, they get their shoes shined. I am out of the ball game with this client." Whenever he found out that a customer played golf, he became "anxious because I know I am on thin ice." It was "disheartening and demeaning," he added, "to know that it doesn't matter how hard I work, how proficient an executive I become, or how successful I become. I will be denied this one benefit that success is supposed to confer on those who have achieved."

Two years after his testimony, Davis told me his obsession with private clubs sprang in part from concerns about his children. Several years before, he had visited a club as a guest and happened to chance upon a white executive he knew. As they were talking, he noticed the man wave at someone on the practice range. It turned out that he had brought his son down to take a lesson from the club pro. Davis was suddenly struck by a depressing thought. "Damn!" he said to himself. "This is being perpetuated all over again. . . . I have a son the same age as his. And when my son grows up he's going to go through the same crap I'm going through if I don't do something about this. His son is learning how to . . . socialize, get lessons, and do business at a country club."

His own son, Davis concluded, would "never ever be able to have the same advantages or even an equal footing."

3 / *Low expectations*. Shortly after I arrived to take over the editorial pages of the New York *Daily News*, I was visited by a black employee who had worked at the paper for some time. More was on his mind than a simple desire to make my acquaintance. He had also come to talk about how his career was blocked, how the deck was stacked against him—how, in fact, it was stacked against any black person who worked there. His frustration and anger I easily understood. But what struck me as well was that his expectations left him absolutely no room to grow. He believed so strongly that the white men at the *Daily News* were out to stymie black achievement that he had no option but failure, whatever the reality of the situation.

Even those who refuse to internalize the expectation of failure are often left with nagging doubts, with a feeling, as journalist Joe Boyce puts it, "that no matter what you do in life, there are very few venues in which you can really be sure that you've exhausted your potential. Your achievement is defined by your color and its limitation. And even if in reality you've met your fullest potential, there's an aggravating, lingering doubt . . . because you're never sure. And that makes you angry."

During the late 1970s, I met a Harvard student, Mark Whitaker, who was interning for a summer in *Newsweek*'s Washington bureau. Whitaker made it clear that he intended to go far. He had it in mind to become editor of *Newsweek*. I didn't know whether to be amused by his arrogance, awed by his ambition, or amazed by his naiveté. I asked Whitaker—the product of a mixed (black/white) union—whether he had considered that his race might hold him back. He answered that maybe it would, but that he was not going to permit his color to smother his aspirations. He would not hold himself back. If he was to be stopped, it would be by someone else.

More than a decade later, when Whitaker had become a *Newsweek* assistant managing editor, I reminded him of our earlier conversation. He laughed his precocious comments off, attributing them to the ignorance and arrogance of youth. We both knew better, of course—just as we knew that many young blacks, for a variety of reasons, never even reach the point of believing that success was within their grasp.

Conrad Harper, former head of the Association of the Bar of the City of New York and a partner in Simpson Thacher & Barlett, said that throughout the years he had seen plenty of young associates "bitterly scarred by not being taken first as lawyers . . . but always first as African Americans." He had also seen affirmative action turned into a stigma and used as a club to beat capable people down. If someone's competency is consistently doubted, "the person begins to question his own abilities." The result, he added, is not only a terrible waste of talent, but in some cases psychological damage.

4 / *Shattered hopes.* After two years toiling at an eminent law firm, the young associate walked away in disgust and became a public defender. For more than a year after leaving, he was "so filled with rage, I couldn't even talk about it much." A soft-spoken Mexican American, he bristles with emotion as he recalls those years.

He believes that he and other minority group hires simply never got a shot at the big assignments, which invariably went to white males. This sense of disappointment, he makes plain, was felt by all the nonwhites in his class. He remembers one in particular, a black woman who graduated with honors from Yale. All her peers thought she was headed for the stars. Yet when she was rated periodically, she was never included in the first tier but at the top of the second.

If he had been alone in his frustration, he says, one could reject his complaint as no more than a case of sour grapes. "But the fact that all of us were having the same kinds of feelings" means something more systemic was at work. He acknowledges that many whites had similar feelings, that in the intensely competitive environment of a top law firm, no one is guaranteed an easy time. But the sense of abandonment, he contends, was exacerbated for nonwhites. By his count, every minority group member who entered the firm with him ended up leaving, having concluded that nonwhites—barring the spectacularly odd exception—were not destined to make it in that world.

5 / *Faint praise*. For a year and a half during the early 1980s, I was a resident fellow at the National Research Council–National Academy of Sciences, an august Washington institution that evaluates scientific research. One afternoon, I mentioned to a white colleague who was also a close friend that it was a shame the NRC had so few blacks on staff. She replied, "Yes, it's too bad there aren't more blacks like you."

I was stunned enough by her comment to ask her what she meant. She answered, in effect, that there were so few really intelligent blacks around who could meet the standards of the NRC. I, of course, was a wonderful exception. Her words, I'm sure, were meant as a compliment, but they angered me, for I took her meaning to be that blacks (present company excluded) simply didn't have the intellect to hang out with the likes of her.

My colleague's attitude seemed to disallow the possibility of a better explanation for the scarcity of blacks than the supposedly low intellectual quality of the race. Perhaps there were so few blacks at the NRC because they simply were not sought out, or because they were encouraged to believe, from childhood on, that they could never master the expertise that would land them in such a place. The ease with which she dismissed such possibilities in favor of a testimonial to my uniqueness disappointed and depressed me.

Blacks who have been singled out as exceptions often experience anger at the whites who commend them. One young woman, a Harvard-trained lawyer with a long list of "firsts" behind her name, had another reason for cringing whenever she was held up as a glistening departure from the norm for her race. "I don't like what it does to my relationships with other blacks," she said.

6 / *Presumption of failure*. A year or so prior to my Harvard Club chat with the *Times* recruiter, I was visited at my office (then in

Berkeley, California) by a *Times* assistant managing editor. I took him to lunch, and after a few drinks we fell into a discussion of people at the *Times*, among them a talented black editor whose career seemed to have stalled. Was he in line, I asked, for a high-level editorship that would soon be vacant? My companion agreed that the editor would probably do very well in the job, but then he pointed out that a black person had never held such a post at the *New York Times*. The *Times* would have to think hard, he indicated, before changing that, for they could not afford to have a black journalist fail in such a visible position. I didn't know whether the man even wanted the job (he later told me he might have preferred something else); I know that he didn't get it, that (at least in the eyes of one *Times* assistant managing editor in 1985) his prior work and credentials could not offset the questions raised by his color. Failure at the highest levels of the *Times* was a privilege apparently reserved for whites.

The *Times'* executive's reasoning reminded me of an encounter with a newspaper editor in Atlanta who had contacted me several years earlier. He had an editorial writer's position to fill and was interested in giving me a crack at it. I was intrigued enough to go to Atlanta and spend an evening with the man. We discovered we shared many interests and friends and hit it off famously. Still, I wondered: Why in the world was he recruiting me? Interesting though Atlanta might be, and as well as he and I got along, there had never been much chance that I would leap at the job. In no way did it represent a career advancement, and the editor's budget would barely permit him to pay the salary I was already making. As the evening wore on, I put the question to him bluntly. Why did he not offer the job to someone in his newsroom for whom it would be a real step up? His answer I found more than a little unsettling. One black person, he said, had already come on staff and not performed very well. He could not afford another black failure, so he had gone after someone overqualified in an attempt to buy himself insurance.

I'm sure he was not surprised that I turned the job down. I was pleased to hear several months later that he had given it to a black reporter already at the paper. Nonetheless, his comments about failure stayed with me long after most of the evening had receded into an alley of fading memories, and I found myself reflecting on them when I recalled a meeting with a newspaper publisher in Chicago years ago.

At the time, I was a very young writer working for the *Chicago Sun-Times*. The editor had invited me and the handful of other black employees to discuss the paper's minority hiring practices with the publisher-owner. The man greeted us warmly but quickly made it plain that he had absolutely no interest in reporters steeped in the "black experience." He wanted journalists who could write and report—presumably about things other than their racial awakening, things he evidently considered well beyond the ability of most blacks. Moreover, he continued, not long ago the paper had hired a black who had been a disaster. To the publisher that apparently constituted a pretty good argument for not going out of his way to hire more blacks. In the face of his attitude, it was hardly necessary to inquire why the paper had never seen fit to move any blacks into its executive ranks.

That discussion took place more than two decades ago, well before the current age of multicultural enlightenment. I doubt it would go the same way today. I don't doubt, however, that similar preconceptions still exist, that before many executives even ask whether a minority person can do a job, they ask whether they are prepared to take a flyer on a probable failure.

7 / *Coping fatigue.* When Armetta Parker headed for Midland, Michigan, to take a job as a public relations professional at the Dow Chemical Company, she assumed that she was on her way to big-time corporate success. A bright, energetic black woman then in her early thirties, Parker had left a good position at a public utility in Detroit to get on the Fortune 100 fast track.

"Dow was everything I expected and more, and everything I expected and less," she says. The town of nearly forty thousand had only a few hundred black families, and virtually no single black people her own age. Though she expected a certain amount of social isolation, "I didn't expect to get the opportunity to take a really hard look at me, at what was important to me and what wasn't." She had to face the fact that success, in that kind of corporate environment, meant a great deal of work and no social life, and that it also required a great deal of faith in people who found it difficult to recognize competence in blacks.

She recalls attending a training session led by a veteran manager who declared, totally out of the blue, that he had absolutely no idea why anyone in a white neighborhood would vote for a certain black mayoral candidate in Chicago. She was the only black in the room and was so troubled by the attitude that seemed to underlie the comment that she walked out.

Nonetheless, Parker did extremely well, at least initially. Her first year at the company, she made it into "The Book"—the roster of those who had been identified as people on the fast track. But eventually she realized that "I was never going to be vice president of public affairs for Dow Chemical." She believed that her color, her gender, and her lack of a technical degree all were working against her. Moreover, "even if they gave it to me, I didn't want it. The price was too high." Part of that price would have been accepting the fact that her race was not seen as an asset but as something she had to overcome. And her positive traits were probably attributed to white genes, she surmised, even though she is no more "white" than most American blacks. Even her way of talking drew attention. Upon meeting her, one colleague remarked with evident pleasure and astonishment, "You don't speak ghettoese." She had an overwhelming sense that what he meant was "You're almost like us, but not enough like us to be acceptable."

After six years she left, without another job in sight: "I was afraid if I stayed one second longer I was going to go off the deep end." For more than a year she traveled and did a variety of short-term stints—as an aerobics instructor, consultant, real estate salesperson—before accepting a job as a press assistant to a U.S. senator. A large portion of her ambition for a corporate career had vanished. She had realized that "good corporate jobs can be corporate handcuffs. You have to decide how high of a price you're willing to pay."

8 / *Pigeonholing*. Near the end of his brashly brilliant tenure as executive editor of the *Washington Post*, Ben Bradlee observed how much both Washington and the *Post* had changed. Once upon a time, he told me, one would not have thought of appointing a black city editor. Now one could not think of *not* seriously considering—and even favoring—a black person for the assignment.

Bradlee, I realized, was making several points. One was about himself and his fellow editors, about how they had matured to the extent that they valued all managerial talent—even in blacks. He was also acknowledging that blacks had become so central to Washington's political, economic, and social life that a black city editor had definite advantages, strictly as a function of race. His third point, I'm sure was wholly unintended but clearly implied: that it was still possible, even for the most enlightened management, to classify jobs by color. And logic dictates that if certain managerial tasks are best handled by blacks, others are best left to whites.

What this logic has meant in terms of the larger corporate world is that black executives have landed, out of all proportion to their numbers, in community relations and public affairs, or in slots where their only relevant expertise concerns blacks and other minorities. The selfsame racial assumptions that make minorities seem perfect for certain initially desirable jobs can ultimately be responsible for trapping them there as others move on.

9 / *Identity troubles*. The man was on the verge of retiring from his position as personnel vice president for one of America's largest companies. He had acquired the requisite symbols of success: a huge office, a generous compensation package, a summer home away from home. But he had paid a price. He had decided along the way, he said matter-of-factly, that he could no longer afford to be black.

I was so surprised by the man's statement that I sat silent for several seconds before asking him to explain. Clearly he had done nothing to alter his dark brown complexion. What he had altered, he told me, was the way he allowed himself to be perceived. Early in his career, he had been moderately outspoken about what he saw as racism within and outside his former corporation. He had learned, however, that his modest attempts at advocacy got him typecast as an undesirable. So when he changed jobs, he decided to disassociate himself from any hint of a racial agenda. The strategy had clearly furthered his career, even though other blacks in the company labeled him an Uncle Tom. He was aware of his reputation, and pained by what the others thought, but he had seen no other way to thrive. He noted as well, with evident pride, that he had not abandoned his race, that he had quietly made it his business to cultivate a few young blacks in the corporation and bring their careers along; and could point to some who were doing very well and would have been doing considerably worse without his intervention. His achievements brought him enough pleasure to balance out the distress of not being "black."

Putting aside for the moment what it means to be "black," the fear of being forced to shed one's identity in order to prosper is not at all uncommon. Georgetown University law professor Anita Allen tells of a worried student who asked whether her diction would have to be as precise as Allen's if she was to be successful as a lawyer. She feared, it seemed, not merely having to change her accent, but being required to discard an important part of herself.

10 / *Self-censorship and silence.* As discussed in the previous chapter, many blacks find their voices stilled when sensitive racial issues are raised. A big-city police officer once shared with me his frustration at waiting nineteen years to make detective. In those days before affirmative action, he had watched, one year after another, as less qualified whites were promoted over him. And each year he had swallowed his disappointment, twisted his face into a smile, and congratulated his white friends as he hid his rage—so determined was he to avoid being categorized as a race-obsessed troublemaker. And he had endured other affronts in silence, including a vicious beating by a group of white cops while carrying out a plainclothes assignment. As an undercover officer working within a militant black organization, he had been given

a code word to whisper to a fellow officer if the need arose. When he was being brutalized, he had screamed out the word and discovered it to be worthless. His injuries had required surgery and more than thirty stitches. When he was asked by his superior to identify those who had beat him, he feigned ignorance; it seems a fellow officer had preceded his commander and bluntly passed along the message that it was safer to keep quiet.

Even though he made detective years ago, and even though, on the side, he managed to become a successful businessman and an exemplary member of the upwardly striving middle class, he says the anger still simmers within him. He worries that someday it will come pouring out, that some luckless white person will tick him off and he will explode, with tragic results. Knowing him, I don't believe he will ever reach that point. But I accept his fear that he could blow up as a measure of the intensity of his feelings, and of the terrible cost of having to hold them in.

11 / *Mendacity.* Even more damaging than self-imposed silence are the lies that seem an integral part of America's approach to race. Many of the lies are simple self-deception, as when corporate executives claim their companies are utterly color-blind. Some stem from unwillingness to acknowledge racial bias, as when people who have no intention of voting for a candidate of another race tell pollsters that they will. And many are lies of business, social, or political convenience, as was the case with Massachusetts Senator Edward Brooke in the early 1970s.

At the time, Brooke was the highest-ranking black politician in America. His name was routinely trotted out as a vice presidential possibility, though everyone involved knew the exercise was a farce. According to received wisdom, America was not ready to accept a black on the ticket, but Brooke's name seemed to appear on virtually everyone's list. During one such period of vice-presidential hype, I interviewed Brooke for a newspaper profile. After asking the standard questions, I could no longer contain my curiosity. Wasn't he tired, I asked, of the charade of having his name bandied about when no one intended to select him? He nodded wearily and said yes, he was.

To me, his response spoke volumes, probably much more than he'd intended. But I took it as his agreement that lies of political convenience are not merely a nuisance for those interested in the truth but a source of profound disgust and cynicism for those on whose behalf the lies are supposedly told.

12 / *Guilt by association*. In the mid 1980s, I was unceremoniously tossed out of Cafe Royale, a restaurant that catered to yuppies in San Francisco, on the orders of a maitre d' who apparently mistook me for someone who had caused trouble on a previous occasion. I sued the restaurant and eventually collected a few thousand dollars from its insurance company. But I will never forget the fury I experienced at being haughtily dismissed by an exalted waiter who would not suffer the inconvenience of having to distinguish one black person from another.

My first real understanding of how poisonous such an attitude could be came to me at the age of twelve or thirteen, when I went to Marshall Field's department store in downtown Chicago in search of a Mother's Day gift. While wandering from one section of the store to another, I gradually became aware that someone was shadowing me. That someone, I ascertained, was a plainclothes security guard. Apparently I fit his profile of a shoplifter. For several minutes, I roamed through the store, trying to ignore him, but he was determined not to be ignored. Little by little, he made his surveillance more obvious, until we were practically walking in lock step. His tactics unsettled me so much that I could no longer concentrate on shopping. Finally, I whirled to face him.

He said nothing, merely glared as my outrage mounted. *How dare he treat me like a criminal*, I thought, *simply because I'm black*. I screamed something at him, I don't remember what. Whatever it was, it had no effect; he continued to stare at me with a look somewhere between amusement and disdain. I stalked out of the store, conceding him the victory, burning with anger and humiliation.

The memory of that day in Marshall Field's came back to me in 1986, when I came across a Richard Cohen column in the

Sunday *Washington Post* magazine that defended the practice of
locking young black men out of Washington boutiques. "Both
blacks and whites believe these young black males are the ones
most likely to bop them over the head," Cohen wrote.

Hundreds of Washingtonians, infuriated by the column and an
accompanying cover-story profile of a black rap artist accused of
murder, demonstrated in protest outside the *Post* building. *Post*
columnist William Raspberry publicly lashed out at his own colleagues. The editors, he wrote, had failed to consider the impact
of publishing an issue of the magazine that "was, in the minds of
thousands of black readers, an indictment of young black men."
Feelings rose to such a pitch that publisher Donald Graham went
on a black-oriented radio station to explain what the *Post* had
been trying to accomplish.

Rudolph Pyatt, a black *Post* business writer, decided to investigate whether the stereotype reflected reality, whether young
black men from the ghetto in fact made up the bulk of those
stealing from Washington stores. He discovered that the youths
were getting a bum rap, that 71 percent of those apprehended for
shoplifting in the area were from middle- and upper-income
households and that more than one-fourth were identified as
"housewives." Pilfering from stores cut so evenly across race and
income lines that experts found it impossible to construct a single
profile of a shoplifter, but they advised Pyatt that a more likely
perpetrator than a young black male was a well-educated middle-
class woman.

In response to the uproar sparked by his article, Cohen wrote
an apologia lamenting that charges of racism had come his way.
By no means, he indicated, was he interested in promoting racist
practices: "I was attempting to point out in my magazine column
that what seems like racism—the refusal to admit or serve young
blacks—is often more complicated than that." He realized that he
was "providing a justification for some racists, but the only way
to avoid that was not to write at all—and that would not have
changed the situation one iota. I wanted very much to get past the
knee-jerk response of racism when certain subjects are raised. To
some extent I succeeded and to some extent I failed."

The view Cohen expressed in his first column is widely accepted. It is view that says that America's cities have become so dangerous, largely as a result of young black thugs, that racial discrimination is justified—and is even a necessary tool of survival when directed at young black men.

Writer D. Keith Mano makes precisely that point in a 1992 piece in the *National Review*. The article describes Mano's narrow escape from a mugger in a New York subway. Upon entering the subway, Mano had spied a "presentable black man . . . thirty or so, just under six foot, trim, in blue track suit and store-white Adidas," lounging on the bottom step. Mano had considered turning back, but something—apparently his resolve to demonstrate racial tolerance—had compelled him to go on. As he had feared, he was attacked, but he jumped into the slimy sludge between the subway tracks and managed to elude his assailant.

His conclusion: "Racism . . . is not always just an illogical, detached, and cruel attitude deriving from callous hate. Racism and hate have their genesis in fear. When that fear is irrational or unexamined . . . then a racist must be held accountable. But, if self-defense can absolve murder, then surely it can absolve racism—*insofar as a person's life is at risk*" (emphasis Mano's). Never again would he be so polite or foolish as to display racial tolerance under such circumstances, "because I'm fifty and too old to jump for my life any more."

In the midst of the Cohen controversy, I mentioned to *Post* publisher Donald Graham that it sounded to me as if Cohen was in fact advocating racism. Graham understandably disagreed, saying Cohen was doing nothing of the sort. Mano, however, makes no bones about the fact that that is exactly what he is advocating *"insofar as a person's life is at risk."*

This rationalization strikes me, to put it mildly, as dangerous. For it inevitably takes one beyond the street, and beyond those black males who are certifiably dangerous. It quickly takes one into society at large, where blacks in no way connected with street crime find themselves victims of street-crime stereotypes. Members of the law-abiding black middle class also have sons, as do those countless African Americans without substantial financial resources who have tried to pound into their children, from birth, that virtue has it rewards, that there is value in following a moral path and shunning the temptations of the street. Mano and Cohen invite the world to treat those young people with contempt. When lives are *at risk*, they apparently deem it perfectly fine to treat every young black man as a criminal until proven otherwise. Not only does that turn the American presumption of innocence on its head, it virtually guarantees that some young men who would otherwise try to become productive citizens will instead become what they are assumed to be. It guarantees, in short, that the number of young black thugs will increase.

To expect "decent black people," in James Q. Wilson's phrase, to accept the idea that they or their sons will be treated like criminals, while also expecting them, as both Wilson and Pete Hamill apparently do, to reach down and uplift the so-called underclass, is to expect, not to put too fine a point on it, one hell of a lot.

Not to say that many will not try. Countless members of the black middle class are in fact volunteering every spare moment in an attempt to do whatever they can (working in homeless shelters, volunteering in literacy programs, serving as formal mentors) to better the lives of those in the so called underclass. At the same time, however, many who belong to America's black privileged class are struggling with problems of their own that are largely unseen or dismissed.

Those problems stem in large measure from assumptions implicit in the reasoning of the James Q. Wilsons of the world, assumptions that acknowledge that stereotyping is a problem but conclude that the fault lies with those who have been wrongly stereotyped. For that is what it means to contend, as Wilson does, that as long "as black men commit violent crimes at a rate that is six to eight times higher than the rate among whites . . . fear will heighten our anxieties and erode our civility" and therefore the "best way to reduce racism real or imagined is to reduce the black crime rate to equal the white crime rate, which, God knows, is high enough."

Wilson's argument is utter nonsense—even if one grants that

the arrest rate (on which his figures are apparently based) is a true reflection of the crime rate. If we were to accept his conclusion about blacks, logic would oblige us to accept various corollary propositions that turn on differences in recorded arrest rates for any number of groups—men and women, for instance.

According to the FBI Uniform Crime Report, in 1990, men, regardless of age, were arrested for violent crimes at levels that dwarfed the numbers for women. Men twenty-five to thirty-four years old were seven times as likely as women in the same age bracket to be arrested for murder, forcible rape, robbery, and aggravated assault. Those from thirty-five to forty-four were seven to eight times as likely to land in jail, and those over sixty-five were nearly fifteen times as likely.

If one applies Wilson's reasoning to those statistics, one would expect discrimination against men to be much more prevalent than discrimination against women. One would expect that until such time as the male crime rate is made to equal the female crime rate, society would treat men as objects of fear and horror. One would expect men, in short, to cure themselves of their evil ways as a condition of acceptance into the world of civil human beings. And one would expect that until men reformed, women would be granted preference in promotion and in hiring, and in apartments and trendy shops, and at every conceivable juncture at which the paths of men and women meet.

To state the argument in these terms is to suggest exactly how ridiculous it is. Yet it is the kind of absurd argument that extremely intelligent people make with perfectly straight faces when discussing the treatment of blacks. And it feeds on the oft-unstated assumption that blacks are still on probation—that unlike white men, who are demonstrably more dangerous than white women (and even more dangerous than black women), blacks are not necessarily granted a presumption of innocence, competence, or even complete humanity. Thus, racial demons are allowed free reign as many Americans, while professing devotion to the ideals of racial harmony, sow seeds that can only yield bitter fruit.

chapter four *A Hostile and Welcoming Workplace*

◆◆◆◆◆◆◆◆◆◆◆◆◆◆◆◆◆◆◆◆◆◆◆◆◆◆◆◆◆

THE EVENING HAD BEEN LONG AND THE DINNER pleasant, with hosts who were a portrait of success. Their suburban home was spacious and tastefully furnished. Their children—three away in college and two in elementary school—were academically accomplished, popular, and athletic. Both parents held advanced degrees from Harvard and were well respected in their fields. For two whose beginnings had been fairly modest, they had more than ample grounds for contentment, even conceit.

As the husband and I sat nursing after-dinner drinks, his cheery mood progressively turned more pensive, and he began to ruminate on his achievements since earning his MBA. By any normal standard, he had done exceedingly well. Within years after graduation, he had risen to a senior position in a national supermarket chain. Shortly thereafter he had taken a job as manager of a huge independent supermarket and had used that as a base from which to launch his own business. He had thought the business would make him wealthy. Instead, he had gone bankrupt, but in the end had landed on his feet with yet another corporate job.

Still, he was not at all pleased with the way his career was turning out. At Harvard, he had always assumed that he would end up somewhere near the top of the corporate pyramid, as had most of his white peers. Yet shortly after graduation he had begun to sense that they were passing him by, so he had opted for the entrepreneurial route. Now that his business had failed and he was again mired in the upper layers of middle-management, he found it galling that so many of his white classmates had prospered with such seeming ease. A considerable number had become corporate royalty, with seven-figure compensation packages, access to private planes, and other accouterments of status and power about which he could only dream. Despite the good life he had, he felt he deserved—and had been denied—so much more.

In the course of conducting interviews for this book, I heard that complaint again and again—not always with the same degree of bitterness or the same doleful sense that opportunity had permanently slipped away, but always with a sadness born of the conviction that for black superachievers success not only came harder but almost invariably later and at a lower level than for comparably credentialed whites.

Wallace Ford, a graduate of Dartmouth College and Harvard Law School, is characteristic. Comparing himself to whites with similar skills, experience, and education, Ford concluded, "I should probably be doing more than I'm doing now." At the time he was New York City's commissioner for business services and, though only in his early forties, had already held a series of impressive-sounding positions: president of the Harlem Lawyers Association, first vice president at Drexel Burnham Lambert Inc., president of the State of New York Mortgage Agency, and others. Still, by his lights, he had underachieved, whether because of "bad luck, bad decisions, race," or "a combination of all three," he wasn't sure. But wherever the primary fault lay, he was certain that race had played a role.

"It's always a factor somewhere," said Ford. "It may not always be up front. It may be in the bushes, or lurking in someone's mind, but it's always there." Not that in the circles he frequented people were likely to vent racial animosities freely. "But you look at a situation and say, *I know.* By having gone to places like Dartmouth and Harvard . . . working with the governor, working with the mayor, [working with] people who are moving up . . . you realize that there's no magic." Yes, some of the stars who had briefly flickered near him before shooting high into the sky were brilliant and extremely well educated, but never so bright that he was "blinded from across the table." So he found himself asking: *Why can they do fifty-million-dollar deals with little more than projections on the back of an envelope?* And why were others, blacks who were "offering to give up mom, dad, and all their kids," able to get only crumbs? "You realize that a lot of it has to do with a lot of factors—race, who you know. Certain people are accorded the opportunity to do X. As you go up the ladder, much is made available to a few."

Even the few blacks who get near the top, who become senior executives in Fortune 500 companies, must ask themselves why they are "not next in line to be chairman [or] CEO of the whole thing," Ford surmised. Just as those brainy blacks who went to top law schools and then found themselves woefully underemployed must ask themselves: *Why?* "My mind cannot accept the fact that of all the [black] people I went to law school with, only half a dozen of them have achieved partnerships in any of the New York law firms."

In his alumni publications, Ford reads of so many whites succeeding so spectacularly, and he wonders why does it not seem to happen for blacks: "With degrees up and down the line, you get jobs, you get opportunities, but you can't achieve any pinnacle that you might think you'd like to compete for." The result is frustration and confusion. "You usually end up suspecting that race is a factor," but the truth is difficult to know. "People aren't saying, 'You black son of a bitch.' " The only real solution, Ford muses, may be for blacks to start more businesses themselves.

Such pessimism from one blessed with so many advantages may strike many readers as strange. But among those of Ford's race and class, his perspective is widely shared.

Darwin Davis, senior vice president with the Equitable Life Assurance Society, came along at a time when opportunities such as those enjoyed by Wallace Ford were all but unimaginable for blacks. After getting his bachelor's degree in business administration from the University of Arkansas in 1954, he returned to his hometown of Flint, Michigan, marched into General Motors headquarters, and inquired about a job. He was told politely but firmly that applications for the management training program were not accepted from "colored people." Devastated, Davis went into the army, then got a master's degree in education and went on to teach mathematics in the Detroit school system. Ten years later, when America's cities erupted in riots, corporations began to open their doors to blacks; Davis got a job at Equitable and did well there. Still, for all the barriers thrown in his way, he believes that those now making their way through the corporate labyrinth may be having an even rougher time. "They have even worse problems because they've got MBAs from Harvard. They went to Princeton. They went to all these places and did all these things that you're supposed to do. . . . And *things* are supposed to happen."

Instead of "things" happening, instead of careers taking off, blacks are being stymied. They are not running into a glass ceiling, says Davis, but into one made of cement and steel. So many young people of his son's generation have about them an "air of frustration" and are surrounded by a wall of gloom "that's just as high now as it was thirty years ago."

Davis's observations are similar to those of management consultant Edward Jones, whose surveys tapped into the frustration raging among black graduates of the nation's top business schools—apparently not a phenomenon that the schools themselves have chosen to explore. Calls to the public relations departments of several of them, including the business schools at Harvard, Stanford, the University of Chicago, and Northwestern, elicited a curious sense of incuriosity about how their minority graduates were faring in the outside world. No one had any idea, I was told again and again, of how well black business graduates were doing relative to whites. But the research being done in the area, carried out largely by black scholars, tends to confirm the perceptions of Ford, Davis, and Jones.

Several years ago, Edward Irons and Gilbert Moore, professors of finance and economics, respectively, conducted a pioneering study of black professionals in banking. The scholars interviewed 125 black bankers in ten different states, distributed one thousand questionnaires (of which nearly one-third were completed and returned) to black bankers in twenty-two states, and reviewed sixteen years' worth of relevant Equal Employment Opportunity Commission statistics. The result was *Black Managers: The Case of the Banking Industry*, published in 1985. Despite the authors' dry prose, their findings were compelling, painting a poignant and depressing picture of the plight of blacks in banking.

Like every other researcher I know of who has asked any large number of black professionals how they are faring, Irons and Moore found a cornucopia of discontent. Interviewees repeatedly complained of being left out of the informal communications network, of "not being in on things." Few reported having "mentors" or anyone high within their organizations who took a supportive interest in their careers. By and large, they judged themselves less likely to be promoted than their white peers and felt they had to expend an inordinate amount of effort trying to make whites "comfortable" with them. They admitted to being under great stress, and many (particularly among the black men in the sample) seemed to be fleeing the field—which led the authors to observe that "black males who have the same high self-image . . . and aggressive personality as white males must either 'walk softly' or face the prospect of being driven out of the industry, out of frustration." Irons and Moore, who had been prepared to find some measure of unhappiness, expressed shock at the magnitude and pervasiveness of the problems they uncovered.

Phyllis Wallace, professor emeritus at Sloan School of Management at the Massachusetts Institute of Technology, reported equally dismal results after systematically examining the experiences of her former students. For five years (from 1980 through 1984), she tracked recent Sloan graduates, trying to compare the progress of blacks and whites who were "similar . . . in every way." She found that virtually from the outset the blacks began to fall behind the whites in terms of income and status in their companies. In part that had to do with the professions they entered. Numerous whites, for instance, went into financial services and management consulting—fields that tended to pay young people extremely well and to promote rapidly during the years of her study. Yet "not a single one of our black students went into the management consulting industry," perhaps, she speculates, because those companies sought employees they thought had potential to attract big-spending clients. Blacks, who "were not seen as able to bring in million-dollar contracts," generally gravitated to Fortune 500 firms.

Once there, said Wallace, they tended to get "stuck in a staff job," and they progressed significantly more slowly than whites. "It was just more difficult for them to be promoted," she observed. "They had to demonstrate over and over again that they were worthy of promotion." Wallace was so concerned by the discrepancies in mobility that she kept in touch with many of the black graduates beyond the period of her research. Eventually, after six or seven years, she found that some received a "double promotion." After initially being held back, they were "finally given the stamp of approval." The result, said Wallace, if not exactly parity with their white classmates, was at least a partial closing of the gap.

Ella Bell, a visiting associate professor at Sloan who has also taught at Yale's school of organization and management, agrees with many of Wallace's findings, but she believes that more recent graduates (unlike those studied by Wallace) have learned to avoid the sinkhole of corporate staff jobs. "The ones that I know of are in bottom-line positions. They are not going into staff positions. . . . They are savvy enough to know you do not do that." What they have not learned, however, is how to stay on the same track as similarly credentialed whites.

"Once they get into these companies, they're astounded," said Bell, "because they feel, 'I went to Yale. I went to Harvard, Sloan, or Stanford. Somehow that's supposed to polish the floor for me so I can just slide on through.' And that does not happen, for a lot of different reasons—race being a factor in that. What usually happens is that blacks will get in with these credentials. They'll make it one or two years, and then all of a sudden they start getting this real fuzzy kind of feedback—what I call static feedback—from their supervisors. Somehow they're 'not good team players.' They're 'too outspoken, too aggressive.' Another favorite one is that 'they 'just don't know how to develop people.' All of this is subjective, nothing that you can fix. . . . And when you ask for examples it gets even flimsier."

As a result, blacks find that "they're not where they want to be. . . . They knew—some of them knew—it was going to be tough." But they also assumed that they would be okay. "Then reality sets in, that they're not going to be okay. They're not getting the positions. They're not getting what was promised . . . a chance to really do some cutting-edge work. So there's a lot of disappointment, and a lot of turnover. . . . A lot of my students, particularly from Yale, [change jobs] within the first two years. One was a brilliant guy from Ghana. He's now gone back to Ghana. . . . I know two others who are looking for jobs right now. It has not turned out the way they thought it would be."

Bell acknowledges that some do "cross over and make it," but they seem to be exceptions to the general rule. And though she believes that white uneasiness with blacks may play some role in black disappointments, the reality is "more complicated." Once upon a time, she recalls, many whites seemed painfully uncomfortable with blacks, "and there are still signs of that. But I've spoken to managers, white males, who are very high up . . . and they talk about having their black colleagues to their homes, to Christmas parties. . . . It's not comfort that's the issue." The issue, as she sees it, is whether those managers are able to see blacks as capable of carrying the company forward, of representing to the company's myriad constituencies the same things white senior executives would represent.

Black women, she believes, face especially daunting challenges, for even as white men are wondering, "Can I really mentor a black female?" black female managers are trying to deflect any suggestion that they may be sleeping with the white boss. For the most part, the women's efforts—at least in that area—seem to be successful. "When I go into companies," said Bell, "I will often hear that white women worked their way up sexually. . . . Very rarely do I hear that about black women." Not that she presumes it to be true when said of white women, but with black women it's rarely even suggested as a possibility: "That's not one of the mythologies you hear."

Sharon Collins, a sociologist with the University of Illinois in Chicago, is no more upbeat than Bell and the others. Collins's professional interest in black managers began in 1980, following

Ronald Reagan's election as president, when she noticed a new anxiety among many black professionals she knew. Blacks who had been doing nicely, "who were driving Mercedes and going to Oak Street and buying suits, . . . were scared—simply because of this change in political administrations." The reason, she concluded after reflection and research, was that for blacks, middle-class status was largely a "politically dependent condition." A disproportionate number of blacks worked for the government, often in "black-related" agencies. Others owed their jobs to "legislation that forced employers to hire blacks." Still others were in positions that "depended on money being funneled from the government into the private sector in all sorts of ways," from job-training programs to minority set asides. If the government had not been looming in the background, "these people would not have been hired for the most part." And with Reagan coming into power, many understandably worried that they would soon lose their tenuous grip on middle-class status.

A few years later (in 1986 and 1987), Collins interviewed seventy-six black senior executives with Fortune 500 companies. She intentionally picked those near the top of the corporate pyramid to see whether blacks at that rarefied level also feared losing their status, and whether they had managed to gain recognition for reasons unrelated to race. "So, essentially, I went to people who actually looked like their white counterparts from all external criteria," said Collins. They had good educations, impressive titles, and huge salaries. But they were also largely pigeonholed by race she discovered. Two-thirds of them had progressed through what she defined as race-related jobs (meaning positions in such areas as affirmative action, community relations, and minority affairs), and half of that number were still in those jobs—even though their titles, in many instances, gave little indication of that.

"There was a constant issue in their careers," said Collins. They were either trying to avoid "black" jobs or trying to get out of them or being penalized for being in them—"because those jobs are going nowhere," and many of those seemingly successful people "won't go one step further than they are now." Indeed, when she returned to interview the executives in 1992, she found that a number had left their companies, a circumstance she attributed largely to the fact that with corporate restructuring proceeding apace, many in minority-related fields were seen as expendable and were let go.

Even among those who were not trapped in race work, Collins found a large measure of discontent. "Very few of them felt really satisfied," she said. "These are ambitious guys, very ambitious, and their eyes are on the prize," yet many were concluding that they were simply not regarded in the same way as their white peers.

Collins recalled one manager who made an especially strong impression on her. "If ever there was a company man, this man is it," she said. He "can hardly say anything without putting it in terms of what's good for the company." Through a long and distinguished career, he had endeavored to earn that company's unconditional respect, clearing every hurdle placed in his path and making every sacrifice required. And he had positioned himself, finally, to reap the rewards of his exertions. But now, despite all his labors, people were passing him by as they moved into jobs he thought he should have. Like many blacks in the same situation, he was having a hard time sorting out whether and to what extent his race was holding him back, but he had reluctantly admitted that racial discrimination was the only explanation that made sense to him.

What did he really want? wondered Collins. "Is it to be seen as if he is white? Or for race not to matter?" If so, "think of how much a black person has to sell of himself to try to get race not to matter. . . . You have to ignore the insults. You have to ignore the natural loyalties. You have to ignore your past. In a sense, you have to just about deny yourself." Collins kept thinking about his pain, she added, and about the price of his denial. "He knows the final threshold is there, and he's losing hope that he can cross it."

Results of a 1991 survey by the Executive Leadership Council were somewhat more upbeat than the bleak portrait painted by Collins and her fellow academics. The council, a Washington-based organization of black executives (most vice presidents or higher at Fortune 500 companies), polled fifty of its fifty-five members and found a bare majority—52 percent—agreeing that their companies created a "comfortable and supportive work environment for African Americans." But even members of this relatively contented group were far from sanguine. Asked to identify the "major restraining force" on their careers, most responded "racism."

"Most executives agreed that the racism they face is covert, elusive, and heavily masked," wrote Jeffalyn Johnson, who analyzed the data for ELC. The survey also found that the executives felt at particular risk of having their careers derailed or of being labeled "troublemakers" if they aggressively promoted the hiring of women and minorities. Johnson concluded that in order to rise, "African-American executives might have to make difficult value decisions between their 'black identity' and orientation and corporate acculturation."

Francine Soliunas, legal counsel for Illinois Bell, has seen black executives cut themselves off from other blacks in their quest to be more acceptable to management. Yet "even those among us who have achieved the ultimate power . . . [are] at some point . . . let know, in some way, shape, or form, that they are [considered] 'nigger[s].' " The message, she says, is transmitted in any number of ways. People quietly make you aware at meetings that they doubt you know what you're talking about. Executives totally outside your area of expertise endeavor to prove that they are more expert than you. The message, as she sees it, is unmistakable, and translates as: "You think you have power? You don't really have power, because I can take away that power anytime I want." As a consequence, even those blacks who are not initially inclined to align themselves with other blacks often end up doing so: "They get religion, if you will. They become part of the networking effort. They speak out more. They are less concerned about the impact in terms of it affecting their positions because their positions have already been affected."

Despite the harshness of her observations, Soliunas is not dissatisfied with her own life. As counsel, her rank is equal to assistant vice president. "I'm comfortable with my level of achievement and my rate of achievement in corporate America," she says. "I've had three promotions in the twelve years I've been here. That's two more than the average lawyer." Nonetheless, she believes that corporate America has violated a morally binding contract, "the contract being if you work, study hard, and excel in your education, and if you work hard and excel on your job, you will have the opportunities—even if you're only that very small fraction that they allow to slip through the gates. I think even those of us who are that small fraction . . . have to recognize that we still confront major, major barriers, even after we've slipped through."

For Soliunas to complain of racism in corporate America even as she expresses satisfaction with her personal achievements is not as contradictory as it may seem. Like other black executives I interviewed, she does not judge her progress in relation to an ideal (and color-blind) standard but in relation to other opportunities in the corporate world. And by that measure she feels she is doing well, particularly in a profession dominated by white males to a greater extent than much of the corporate world.

"Typically corporate lawyers . . . are the white-haired, three-piece black-pin-striped-suit gentlemen," says Soliunas. "They are not little chubby black women who have white-haired, three-piece-suit-wearing gentlemen as their clients. And so, on any number of occasions in working for Illinois Bell, I've walked into court with my clients and the judge immediately starts directing his questions to my clients on the assumption that they're the lawyer and I'm the client."

Gender, race, and raiment incongruities notwithstanding, Soliunas is confident that many of her white colleagues recognize her talents and give her credit for her accomplishments. But she also senses from some of them an attitude of " 'How dare you to put yourself on the same plane with me! How dare you to challenge me! How dare you to think that you have the option to question my power and my authority!' And I think it's very subtle. . . . It's communicated . . . when there's a meeting and there are discussions going on and you express a dissenting opinion. Or you challenge someone who is deemed to be the authority on the issue. . . . I see a very different reaction from my challenging them than I've seen with white females. . . . I don't see it with a lot of white men. It's not a pervasive attitude. But it is an attitude and it is present in white males of power who can influence your career.''

Soliunas, who came to Illinois Bell after working as a litigator in county, state, and federal government, acknowledges that her career in the private sector did not get off to the most auspicious start. Before her first promotion, two white males were moved up. A white female and two other white males advanced along with her. All the males were promoted to higher positions, all had been at the company for less time than she, and all had less experience as lawyers. She is not certain that race accounts for her slower start. A number of plausible reasons could be offered, including the fact that at the time her area of specialization was not sufficiently broad. But ''no one took me by the hand and said, 'You know, you've got to move out of labor now if you want to move into a [higher] position.' ''

Soliunas finds fulfillment not only in having risen in the company, but in helping others. ''My satisfaction comes from knowing that I have positioned myself in a way that allows me to have a tremendous amount of power in terms of being able to impact policy in a number of ways, but specifically with respect to minorities in the corporation. . . . If there is a decision to terminate, a decision that may negatively impact a minority or a female, a decision that has to do with money, particularly compensation that may have some negative impacts, I'm the one that they talk to.'' But getting there wasn't easy, and ''when it happened for me, it happened very late in the game.''

Basil Paterson, the former deputy mayor of New York, makes a similar point more poignantly. ''Every day I realize that I'm further ahead than I ever thought I would be in my life,'' yet ''by any standard that is uniquely American, I'm not successful. It's too late for me to get rich because I spent too much time preparing for what I've got. . . . Most of us are ten years behind what we should have been. We couldn't get credentials until we were older than other folks.'' And he is not at all sure that the next generation will have it much better. He recently received a résumé from a black graduate of a prestigious law school who claimed she wanted experience in international commerce. "She can't get international commerce working for me," Paterson pointed out, speculating that she had come to him because she saw few opportunities elsewhere.

Certainly, in law—as in other professions—when blacks are asked how they are doing, they consistently say they are not doing nearly as well as whites tend to assume. In 1992, when the Association of the Bar of the City of New York surveyed minority associates at the city's major law firms, the pollsters found that blacks in particular felt isolated and neglected.

Largely as a result of the efforts of Conrad Harper, president of the association, 169 law firms and corporate law departments had signed a "Statement of Goals" the previous year pledging to improve retention and promotion rates for nonwhites and calling for a 10 percent minority hiring rate between 1992 and 1997. The 1992 survey, conducted by a subcommittee of the Committee to Enhance Professional Opportunities for Minorities charged with implementing that agreement, was far too small to yield firm generalizations, including only twenty-three blacks, twenty-one Asian-Americans and Pacific Islanders, nine Hispanics, three "others," and three who did not give their race. Nevertheless, its findings were consistent with the stories I heard in my own research, and with virtually every survey I have seen that has tried to assess the feelings of black professionals. And the picture it painted was sobering.

Sixty-one percent of blacks felt their work experiences were "clearly different from [those of] nonminority lawyers" at their firms. Only 9.5 percent of Asians/Pacific Islanders and none of the Hispanics felt that way. Thirty percent of the blacks said they were "judged differently from nonminority lawyers," with another 30 percent unsure. Only 20 percent unequivocally said they were judged in the same way compared to 89 percent of the Hispanics and 76 percent of the Asians/Pacific Islanders. Sixty-one percent of blacks thought their firms had a poor "commitment to the retention of minority lawyers," as did 67 percent of Hispanics and 29 percent of Asians/Pacific Islanders.

In a statement released with the survey, Harper said: "The implication of this modest, not scientific yet persuasive survey, augmented by the undeniable lack of advancement of African-American lawyers to the partnership level, is that such lawyers perceive far more race-related barriers to their professional development than do other minority lawyers. . . . To communicate openly across cultures requires a comfort level that does not presently seem to exist in law firms."

That observation was driven home by an accompanying bar association report, which stated, "Most law firms, no doubt, believe that they have created an environment in which the perceptions described in the survey would be unwarranted. However, the fact that these perceptions may come as a surprise is explained by some of the comments made in follow-up interviews. . . . A third generation African-American lawyer described himself as not feeling 'entitled to complain' because he was 'lucky to be there.' "

Harper, the first African American elected to head the association, was made a partner in Simpson Thacher & Barlett in 1974. At the time, there were only two other black partners in major New York law firms. Over the years, the number has climbed to more than thirty. And through that entire period, Harper said, he had often heard black associates complain of being treated "differently." He and the handful of other black partners saw the bar association's foray into survey research as part of a process of making the profession "more hospitable to blacks and other minorities," and of underlining the point that simply hiring blacks associates was not the same as putting them on an equal footing with whites.

That Harper, Francine Soliunas, Sharon Collins, and the others quoted above should find so much evidence of corporate inhospitality to blacks may be a matter of skewed perceptions, or of what Senator Moynihan insists is a tendency of middle-class blacks to wallow in a "legacy of grievance . . . inappropriate to their condition." Another possibility is that the grievances are real: that corporate America, in ways more persistent and pervasive than most whites realize, is playing a cruel trick on those who thought they could escape the curse of discrimination simply by adhering to the rules; that what the would-be trailblazers discover is that following the rules carries few guarantees—for those of any race; that while a good education, hard work, and high performance can increase the odds of success, a host of other factors, having nothing to do with ability or merit, ultimately dictates how high one can rise; and that those other factors often differ as a function of race.

Part of the problem, as management consultant Edward Jones pointed out, is that though Americans constantly "talk about merit . . . we can't even define what it is." Outside of sports and certain technical specialties, merit tends to be defined subjectively, primarily by attaching complimentary labels to those who are thought to be meritorious: people who are "fast starters," who "have potential," who show style or demonstrate leadership or otherwise have the mystical "right stuff" that will take them to the top. Once they have risen, as predicted, it is assumed they did so on merit—a reassuring if circular assumption. But what it fails to take into account is the real possibility that merit, objectively defined, has relatively little to do with who gets ahead.

A 1984 study by sociologist James Rosenbaum (published as *Career Mobility in a Corporate Hierarchy*) took a hard look at career advancement in one large company. Rosenbaum, who had full access to personnel records, tracked one cohort's progress through the corporation over a thirteen-year period. In the end, he had processed some 20 million discrete pieces of data and had concluded that careers developed very differently—and along much narrower tracks—than generations of management had assumed.

Whereas management (and employees) believed that good work could be rewarded at any stage of a career, Rosenbaum found that early job assignments and early promotions had an enduring influence "independent of the most salient individual attributes." In other words, those who were designated as "fast starters" did significantly better throughout their careers than others—irrespective of actual ability or performance. He also discovered that people tended to be categorized very quickly, often before they were aware of it. "Even employees who were on the fast track learned about it gradually. . . . They reported noticing the extra attention they were receiving, they began to infer that they were getting special treatment, and later they realized that they were advancing more quickly than their peers."

This process, noted Rosenbaum, was in important respects just the opposite of the meritocracy many assumed to be operating. For if there is to be true equality of opportunity within a corporation, "employees must know the rules of the game, they must start at similar positions, and they must be allowed to begin the tournament when they are ready to compete." His findings, he said, "raise doubts about each of these points." He added that a system that tracked employees so early in the process was "particularly weak at discovering errors of exclusion. It does not have any way to bring former losers back into the competition for top positions." The likelihood of worthy employees being excluded was compounded, he observed, in "sponsored" programs, in which management selects workers presumed to have high potential and moves their careers along. Yet many large corporations, and certainly most major law firms, operate in precisely this way.

Conrad Harper, for instance, recalls that early in his career he did not realize that he was being groomed for success until one of his firm's eminences pulled him aside and told him he would be working very closely with a certain senior partner. "There is no such thing as a self-made partner in a major law firm," Harper says. "One cannot advance in places like this without a godfather." But as Rosenbaum found, a system based on mentorship, or on early tracking of future corporate stars, "carries the risk that the term 'high-potential people' does not so much describe a type of person as it describes a predefined role to which some individuals will be assigned regardless of their personal qualities."

Some of Rosenbaum's research was foreshadowed by sociologist Robert Merton, who explained the concept of the "self-fulfilling prophecy" in a famous article in *the Antioch Review* in 1948. His inspiration came from W. I. Thomas's observation that "if men define situations as real, they are real in their consequence." A series of studies in the 1960s and 1970s explored the concept in the classroom and found, at least in some instances, that student performance seemed to be largely shaped by teacher expectations. According to Ray Rist, who investigated a predominantly black school in St. Louis, "If the teacher expects high performance, she receives it, and vice versa." He found that once students were tracked into ability groups—largely on the basis of appearance and dress—there was virtually no movement either up or down.

Rosenbaum's study, an analysis of general career mobility, was radically different from Rist's, but he too found that once people were put into tracks, they tended to stay in them. And while his research was not designed to look specifically at race, his findings have clear racial implications. If in fact blacks tend to be tracked into certain areas, and if in fact blacks are therefore destined to progress more slowly than whites, and if in fact the real reasons for advancement have less to do with ability than with attributes one is *a priori* assumed to possess, then it is only to be expected, given certain widespread racial assumption in America, that very few blacks, however accomplished, manage to get near the top of the corporate hierarchy.

Furthermore, if in fact many whites get ahead in large part because they are beneficiaries of a congenial stereotype (which presupposes that executives and corporate lawyers are white), of early high-profile job assignments (which whites are more likely to get), of mentors (whom whites have an easier time acquiring), and of wide latitude to fail (but also to triumph), then it should not be much of a mystery why even those blacks who do get into corporate management sometimes feel so bitter.

In career development, as Rosenbaum notes, the loss of even a few years can be critical. And yet, if the testimony of those I interviewed is to be believed, blacks almost automatically lose the years it typically takes to make a corporation comfortable with them. By the time the corporation finally does become comfortable and acknowledges abilities, the fast trackers (who are almost always white) have already moved on—so that even the most talented blacks often end up in slower lanes. When someone like Basil Paterson says, "It's too late for me," he is not speaking for himself alone, but for thousands upon thousands of other blacks who wonder how much better they would be doing in a fairer world.

If the phenomenon of the false meritocracy were a thing of the past, Moynihan's dismissal of black middle-class discontent would make a great deal of sense. But the little evidence that exists on blacks with fast-track credentials indicates that for whatever reason, they generally are not getting on the track, certainly in nothing approaching the proportions of their white peers. And given all the stories of disappointed young achievers who walk away from corporations in disgust, like Professor Bell's black MBAs, it seems premature, at the very least, to pronounce their problems little more than figments of their collective imagination.

This is not to say that blacks are altogether faultless. As Illinois Bell's Francine Soliunas put it, "I don't think it is all corporate America's making. I think we have had opportunities to perhaps build stepping stones to that [glass] ceiling to break through and we've choked . . . by not learning what it is that we have to do in order to break though, and not being willing to do it because of some fear, real or imagined, that we will compromise our blackness or our femininity, or whatever else it is." Nor am I arguing that corporations or major law firms are openly hostile to blacks. Naked hatred and open hostility are—thank God—largely relics of a wretched past. Still, many institutions and the individuals within them have trouble seeing blacks in the same light in which they customarily see whites.

Ross Perot demonstrated that in 1992 when he addressed the national convention of the NAACP and persisted in referring to blacks as "you people," dwelling on anecdotes of his parents' personal kindnesses to black hobos and blue-collar employees. No one accused Perot of being a racist—if a racist is defined as one who hates another racial group. What he was charged with was unwitting condescension, with assuming that simply because his audience was black, it would relate to stories about black bums—which implied that in Perot's mind the most important bond between members of the audience was an interest in the benevolence of whites towards blacks. It is hardly conceivable, for instance, that he would have addressed middle-class whites as "you people" or regaled them with stories of his father's generous treatment of tramps, whatever their color.

Corporate America is full of people like Perot, people who, without intending to create racial hurdles or hostility, manage to create a fair amount of both. That they cannot see what they have done is due partly to the fact that they meant no harm and partly to a disinclination to examine whether the assumptions they hold dear are in accord with reality.

In December of 1992, in an elegy for the demise of the marriage of the Prince and Princess of Wales, the *New York Times* editorialized, "On July 29, 1981, millions of Americans rose at dawn to watch a young woman who actually looked like a princess (golden hair, blue eyes, and a whopper of a tiara) marry a prince who didn't exactly look like one (he's no Tom Cruise). But what the heck. The music was swell, St. Paul's Cathedral never looked better and, all in all, it was the kind of wedding that even money can't buy." No one with any sense would argue that running a major American corporation is equivalent to being the Prince of Wales, but senior corporate executives and senior partners in law firms are also expected to conform to a certain image. And though their positions may not require golden hair and blue eyes, they do require the ability to look like—and be accepted as—the ultimate authority. To many Americans that image still seems fundamentally incongruous with kinky hair and black skin.

chapter five *Crime, Class, and Cliches*

◆◆◆◆◆◆◆◆◆◆◆◆◆◆◆◆◆◆◆◆◆◆◆◆◆◆◆◆◆◆

W̌HATEVER DIFFICULTIES AMERICANS MAY HAVE thinking of blacks as potential CEOs, no particular imagination is required to visualize crime with an African-American face. In every major city in this country, blacks accused of the most heinous offenses routinely stare from front pages and television screens into middle America's living rooms. Those chilling, even monstrous images have come to represent, in many minds, the predominant reality of black America; and they have come, to an enormous extent, to color attitudes toward race relations, and toward all members of the race.

During a visit to Washington, D.C., in early 1993, I happened to spot former *Washington Post* executive editor Benjamin Bradlee on the street. I instructed my taxi driver to stop, Bradlee hopped in, and during the ensuing conversation I told him I was completing a book about race. Bradlee sighed and confessed that he was worried about what race was doing to him, that his home had been broken into more than once, and that he now found he was scared all the time. Tellingly, though I had said nothing at all about crime, it was his first association when the subject of race was broached.

Daniel Patrick Moynihan puts the point with characteristic bluntness: "If black continues to mean crime in cities, it won't help you to be a summer intern at Skadden Arps [a major New York–based law firm] pulling down twenty-three hundred dollars a week just to be taken to lunch." James Q. Wilson, as noted previously, makes the same case. Indeed, Moynihan was so impressed with Wilson's articulation of the "best way to reduce racism . . . is to reduce the black crime rate" thesis that he read it into the *Congressional Record.*

Former New York Mayor Edward Koch takes a similar—if more simplistic—position. Koch contends that "even those who feel deeply about discrimination against blacks . . . feel estranged from the black community" as a consequence of "black violence." According to Koch's calculation, blacks, who make up 12 percent of the population, are committing 45 percent of violent crimes. And since "for the most part only males are committing the crimes of violence . . . roughly 6 percent of the population is committing 45 percent of the crimes." Even if one accepts Koch's statistics, one must judge his conclusion preposterous, for it would mean that every black male in America—the 6 percent in his equation—is engaged in acts of mayhem. In other words, even black lawyers, accountants, teachers, and salesmen who put in long hours at work are apparently getting their jollies (during their lunch breaks, one supposes) by cracking hapless innocents over the head or "wilding" in big-city parks.

It is true, as Koch indicates, that blacks account for about 45 percent of those arrested for America's violent crimes. But it is not true that most black males are vicious. FBI statistics show that blacks were arrested 245,437 times in 1991 for murder, forcible rape, robbery, and aggravated assault. The country's total population then was just under 249 million, including nearly 31 million blacks and roughly 15 million black males. If we assume that each arrest represents the apprehension of a separate individual, blacks arrested for violent crimes made up less than 1 percent of the black population in 1991—and just under 1.7 percent of the black male population (less, in fact, since the aggregate figure of 245,437 includes crimes committed by females). In other words, less than one-tenth of a percent of the population—*not 6 percent*—is committing 45 percent of violent crimes. These numbers are not completely accurate, since the FBI population base is somewhat smaller than the entire U.S. population, and since it is not correct to infer that those arrested in any one year make up the total population of violent criminals. But they are accurate enough to show the inanity of implying that most black males are sociopaths.

To many thoughtful people, certainly to many blacks, arguments like Koch's seem not only absurd but fundamentally unfair. For they suggest that discrimination against an entire race, if not exactly sanctioned, is acceptable because of the sins of a relative few. They also suggest that blacks who do not commit crimes bear a special responsibility for those who do.

Many law-abiding African Americans react viscerally to such suggestions. Ulric Haynes, dean of Hofstra University's business school, declares, "Among my circle of black friends, who by anybody's standards would be overachievers, every one of us is concerned for the so-called underclass and, in some way or another, is involved in helping. . . . I have gotten our school of business involved in a partnership relationship with the Hempstead school district—which is overwhelmingly black and Latino, and is horribly poor in terms of quality—in curriculum redesign, in trying to get them computer equipment to upgrade their business education program, in one-on-one relationships." Yet he has no intention of buying into the proposition that the middle class should be responsible for the well-being of the black underclass and penalized for the transgressions of the black criminal class. "For me to accept that, they would also have to acknowledge that there's poor white trash, that there're rednecks, that there're pockets of white poverty where people behave outrageously. And until they do that, I'm not willing to accept the burden of my black brethren who behave outrageously. . . . In every society there are the underdogs and there is an underclass. And I am not going to take on the black underclass as a special burden of mine as a black man, although I am concerned. And I will demonstrate my concern. But don't hang that one on me."

Haynes's point is not easily dismissed. These days, no serious thinker in the field of criminal justice would propose that the answer to violent crime among whites is for up-and-coming white executives to make crime prevention their special mission. Nor would anyone propose, for instance, that until the murder rate among twenty-something whites was made to equal the murder rate among seventy-something whites, all young whites deserved to be ostracized and scorned. And certainly no reasonable person would dare suggest that since organized crime has historically been run largely by Italians and Italian Americans, and since people are afraid of organized crime, we should discriminate against all Italian Americans until Italian criminals become part of polite society. Not even most bigots would argue that since the Mafia is dominated by Italians, crime is an "Italian problem" that can only be solved by Italians. No one would seriously put forth such an approach because virtually everyone would immediately recognize it as the promotion of unreasoned prejudice. Yet that is precisely the approach many reputable people are now recommending in regard to blacks. And it is a most pernicious proposition. To contend that we should penalize all members of a racial or ethnic group because some members are engaged in egregious behavior is to enter into a pact with the devil whose evil has no end.

Nonetheless, because the argument has assumed such importance in so many minds, it cries to be addressed—as Bill Bradley did in a Senate floor speech in March 1992. "Never mind that in a society insufficiently color-blind all black men have to answer for the white fear of violence from a few black men. Never mind that Asian Americans fear both black and white Americans, or that in Miami or Los Angeles, some of the most feared gangs are Latinos and Chinese. Never mind that the ultimate racism was whites ignoring the violence when it wasn't in their neighborhoods, or that black Americans have always feared certain white neighborhoods. . . . Today, many whites responding to a more violent reality . . . see young black men traveling in groups, cruising the city, looking for trouble, and they are frightened. Many white Americans, unfairly or fairly, seem to be saying of some young black males, "You litter the street and deface the subway, and no one, black or white, says stop. . . . You rob a store, rape a jogger, shoot a tourist, and when they catch you, if they catch you, you cry racism. And nobody, white or black, says stop." It matters not, he added, whether the image is accurate. "It is what millions of white Americans feel is true. In a kind of ironic flip of fate, the fear of brutal white repression felt for decades in the black community and the seething anger it generated now appear to be mirrored in the fear whites have of attack from blacks and the growing anger it fuels.''

When I spoke to Bradley several months after his speech, he again commented on the irony that blacks—who for so long feared violence from whites—should now find themselves the object of fear. And he wondered aloud, if black violence was the rationale for unequal treatment of all blacks, how such treatment could have been justified in, say, 1905, when whites essentially had nothing to fear from blacks.

Political scientist Andrew Hacker makes the same point. ''Prior to World War II, when lawbreaking by blacks was relatively rare, communities still posted these signs: NIGGER, DON'T LET THE SUN SET ON YOU IN THIS TOWN!'' Indeed, throughout the history of blacks in America, from slavery on, antiblack sentiments have flourished, and their expression often did not end with the posting of a sign.

In the early part of the nineteenth century, riots broke out in Philadelphia, Cincinnati, and several other cities as white mobs attacked blacks for alleged offenses against whites—in an era when merely raising one's voice could be considered a grave offense. America's worst race riot ever, in 1863, was perpetrated by whites (largely Irish immigrants) who, in the period following the Emancipation Proclamation, felt economically threatened by blacks exempted from the military draft. The mobs roamed through Manhattan, at one point setting fire to the Orphan Asylum for Colored Children, whose several hundred residents barely escaped with their lives. Rioters lynched, knifed, and mutilated blacks at random. The terrifying rampage caused the city's blacks to seek shelter wherever they could find it—including in the foliage of Central Park and out of state.

Attacks against blacks did not cease with the end of the Civil War, or even with the end of the nineteenth century. Lynchings and other mass forms of antiblack violence occurred well into the twentieth century. In Statesboro, Georgia, in 1904, white mobs burned two black men alive. Two years later, in Atlanta, whites stormed black homes and businesses. In 1908, a white mob in Springfield, Illinois, hanged two blacks and destroyed black-owned property. In East St. Louis, in 1917, white rioters killed forty blacks and destroyed several hundred homes. In 1919, anti-black violence broke out across the country, with the worst eruption taking place in Chicago. Much of the violence stemmed from one of two fears: either that blacks would take jobs from whites or that blacks returning from war would demand rights the country was not prepared to grant. Toward the end of World War II, a new wave of antiblack mob violence broke out in the South as well as in the North, with riots in Mobile, Alabama, Beaumont, Texas, and Detroit.

Rarely in the early part of this century were whites punished for terrorizing blacks. According to legal scholar James Chadbourn, fewer than 1 percent of the whites who lynched some two thousand blacks between 1900 and 1935 were arrested and convicted. Decades later, even as the civil rights movement swept the country, activists discovered that old ways died hard—as illustrated by the acquittal in 1957 of two whites accused of bombing a black church in Montgomery, Alabama.

In *Caste and Class in a Southern Town,* a brilliant book first published in 1937 (and so admired by Moynihan that he wrote an effusive foreword to the fiftieth-anniversary edition, with which he presented me upon learning of my research), John Dollard repeatedly and eloquently made the point that only whites—at least in the town he studied—were permitted to be interracially aggressive. One reason many white men focused on black women as sexual objects, Dollard suggested, was that "the Negro man is debarred from violent expressions or threats in defending his wife, sister, or daughter." At another point he observed, "Every Negro in the South knows that he is under a kind of death sentence; he does not know when his turn will come, it may never come, but it may also be at any time. This fear tends to intimidate the Negro man." Dollar went on to recount an incident illustrating the "atmosphere of intimidation." Accompanied by several white men, he went to see some black sharecroppers: "The car pulled up in front of a cabin, and the driver called out to a Negro man on the porch, 'Hey, Bill, come here.' The Negro seemed apprehensive and the driver called back, 'Come on, we are not going to hang you,' and laughed. We went to three or four cabins and in every one the same little drama occurred. The Negroes were frightened and reluctant. They did not know what might happen when four white men drove up in a car before their place. Any situation involving unknown white men looks ominous to the Negro. I commented to the driver that 'the Negroes seem to be very polite around here,' and he answered with a laugh, 'They have to be.' "

Well after Dollard wrote those words, blacks continued to be the target of white violence. Yet at no point in the long history of antiblack aggression did any widely respected scholar suggest that wholesale retaliation against innocent whites was justified. Or that until the white crime rate was reduced, all whites should be subject to discrimination. Or that law-abiding whites should accept a special burden, or bear a special guilt, because of the actions of their less disciplined brethren. Yet those who now so glibly urge law-abiding blacks to take responsibility for (or at least accept the consequences of) crimes committed by black hoodlums see nothing at all bizarre, irrational, or inconsistent in the proposal.

There is little point in quibbling here over whether arrest statistics—from which crime rate figures are derived—are skewed by the possibly discriminatory acts of arresting officers. Or whether the National Crime Survey (which is based on interviews with victims and shows less discrepancy between blacks and whites for certain types of violent crime) is really a better measure of violent offenses. Or whether discrimination in the judicial system results in blacks being disproportionately convicted of crimes. I do not dismiss any of those arguments; but I accept it as true for all practical purposes that African Americans, taken as a group, commit more violent crimes on average than white Americans. That fact, however, is hardly remarkable. For one thing, blacks are more likely to be unemployed (whether because of discrimination or other factors is irrelevant in this context). Blacks have also been instructed—and I suspect that this is crucial—by the media, by other blacks, and by the random reactions of strangers, that they are expected to be criminals.

But even granting a higher black crime rate, it makes no apparent sense to assume that anything good will come of telling blacks who have rejected violence that their efforts are pointless, that no matter what values they hold and no matter how they behave, they will be treated like muggers until the black crime rate goes down. That is less a crime reduction strategy than a prescription for hopelessness and frustration—and an incentive for turning away from lawful conduct. Yet that is what many intellectuals, shopkeepers, and self-styled philosophers are now telling the black middle class.

Bill Bradley recalls an incident from the late 1970s when a black friend of his, a second-year student at Harvard Law School, was interning at a major Los Angeles firm. Every Sunday a partner would have brunch at his home, to which the interns would be invited. One Sunday, his friend was en route with a white woman, who Bradley believes was also an intern, when he was stopped by the police. Suddenly the friend was pulled from his car, surrounded, thrown to the ground, and handcuffed as a police officer ran over to the woman and said, "You're being held against your will, aren't you?" After fifteen or twenty minutes, the two interns managed to satisfy the policemen that the black man was not a rapist or a kidnapper, and he was finally allowed to return to his car. The police left without a word of explanation or apology. For Bradley, the incident illustrates how problematic it is to proceed from the assumption that any black male is a criminal. "A lot of African Americans who have not only no relation to the violence, but are in the foreground of fighting the violence, are getting hit because of the violence," he says. Given that fear of crime is rampant among both blacks and whites, "this should be an issue that unites."

The merit in Bradley's argument is obvious. If the problem is crime, common sense dictates that we come up with a solution that addresses crime, not one that indiscriminately punishes criminals and the innocent alike. The practice of locking every black person out of a jewelry shop may reduce the odds of a robbery, but it will also create a reservoir of bitterness in blacks who approach the door with nothing more than a purchase in mind. If the objective is to eliminate stickups, it would make more sense to take aggressive action against stickups—even if that means con-

ducting business from behind bulletproof glass and armor plate—
than to insult all black prospective customers who attempt to
enter. Moreover, if harsh treatment of even law-abiding blacks is
to be the preferred approach to fighting crime, the price paid for
being black may not end with an insult.

A policeman friend of mine made that point one evening as he
discussed his dilemma over his son, a recent college graduate
whom he wanted to install in a successful business he had started
during his off hours. Yet he was reluctant to ask his son to come
to New York because he was afraid of the city's violence. At first
I assumed he meant the violence of the heavily armed hoodlums
who have become such a fixture on urban streets, but as he went
on, it became clear that the violence he feared was not from the
city's criminals but from its cops. He had been in enough ugly
situations with fellow officers, he explained, to know that some of
them simply took it for granted that any young black man they
encountered was scum. Because of that preconception, and also
because his son was not particularly meek, my friend envisioned
nothing but trouble if a certain type of cop happened to stop his
son on the street. Struck by the turn the conversation had taken,
I didn't say much. Instead, I listened; and what I heard was the
outrage and anguish of a black cop who was also a father and who
had witnessed what happened when decent young black men
were taken for thugs by cops intent on teaching them a lesson.
Those who were beaten first and questioned later were in his
experience almost always black or Latino. And he had seen it
happen often enough that even though he knew the odds were
against his son's becoming such a casualty, he could not dismiss
the possibility.

Several months following that conversation, the issue of police
behavior toward black men—particularly young black men—was
very much on many New Yorkers' minds because of the shooting
of a black transit policeman by white colleagues who mistook him
for a mugger or a thief. The "friendly fire" incident began after
the black plainclothes cop and his white partner chased a woman
suspect and cornered her on a dark street. The black officer,
Derwin Pannell, was guarding her, and his partner was going

through her purse, when three other transit cops—two male, one female, all white—chanced upon them.

At this point, the stories of the officers who opened fire and of the one who was shot differ dramatically. They claimed they shouted a warning. He said they did not. They claimed he turned with his weapon drawn. He said he did not. At any rate, two opened fire, one with a fifteen-shot semiautomatic and the other with a .38 six-shooter. Both emptied their weapons. (The one woman cop on the scene held her fire.) Most of the bullets went wild. Two hit Pannell's bulletproof vest without doing major damage. A third hit him in the neck and left him partially paralyzed.

All the white cops insisted that race was not a factor in the shooting. Pannell himself subsequently indicated that while his race may have played a part, poor police training—not racism—was to blame. But Eric Adams, an official of the Guardians, a predominantly black police association, insisted that the racial aspect could not be dismissed. "Too many people in this department can't tell a black cop from a black criminal," he said when I spoke to him, as officials grappled for an explanation for the sad turn of events. Adams feared for black officers' safety: there was rarely a problem when cops came upon a white male in plain clothes, but "when you see a male black [you] have negative perceptions because you live in a society with negative perceptions."

In response to the Pannell incident and the Guardians' concerns, transit officials promised better training in undercover procedures and in dealing with minority suspects in ambiguous and potentially dangerous situations. Adams saw this as a triumph. Not only would it make black officers feel safer, but it had strong symbolic significance. "For the first time," he said, "a major law enforcement agency agreed they didn't have all the answers . . . and will reach out to African-American cops." In acknowledging that they could learn something important from their black officers, transit police authorities had also acknowledged that perhaps black cops faced a threat that most white cops did not.

Black police officers in many American cities share the concerns of their counterparts in New York. Once stripped of the protective coloration of their uniforms, they say, they can end up on the wrong side of a fellow officer's nightstick or gun. The month after the Pannell incident, that belief was given credence when five white officers beat a black colleague in Nashville. The black plainclothesman, Reginald Miller, was investigating prostitution when the white cops stopped him for a minor traffic violation, held a gun to his head, and roughed him up.

One of the more bizarre incidents involving a black out-of-uniform officer occurred in 1989, when Don Jackson, a police sergeant from Hawthorne, California, went to nearby Long Beach to investigate rumors of police abuse. Jackson was affiliated with a nonprofit agency called the Police Misconduct Lawyer Referral Service, which claimed to have received scores of complaints about the Long Beach police assaulting minority residents. Accompanied by an off-duty federal corrections officer, Jackson drove through Long Beach in casual clothes, trailed by an unmarked NBC television van with a camera crew he'd invited along. His sedan was pursued by two white Long Beach policemen who pulled him over for no apparent reason and ordered him out of the car. Swearing at Jackson while ordering him to submit to a weapons search, one of the officers shoved his head through a plate glass window and threw him onto the police car.

Later, in a *New York Times* op-ed piece, Jackson addressed the consequences of equating black skin with criminality. He was "well aware" that black criminals existed, and was fully prepared to fight them, but he also recognized "that blacks are labeled criminal at birth." Police often brutalize blacks "whether we are complying with the law or not," he charged. "We have learned that there are cars we are not supposed to drive, streets we are not supposed to walk. We may still be stopped and asked 'Where are you going, boy?' whether we're in a Mercedes or a Volkswagen."

The situation of the black undercover officer is in some ways unique. Few other respectable Americans of any race are likely to be found toting guns on city streets or succeeding at their professions by looking like thugs. And few black Americans who are not in law enforcement can simply change clothes and protect themselves—as long as they are in uniform—from being taken for common crooks, from being stripped of all status by a smug voice asking, "Where are you going, boy?" ("May I help you?").

Several years ago, I was stopped in northern California by two white policemen who said they were looking for a burglar. The encounter was not particularly unpleasant, and I never had the sense of being in physical danger. Indeed, once they saw my nice conservative suit and the impressive title on my business card, they quickly concluded they had the wrong man. They were after a person fitting my description, but no one "who would be wearing a suit like yours." They apologized and explained that I had looked "suspicious" sitting in my car outside a certain building. I had dropped a friend at the building on the way home from work and waited outside long enough to see her turn the light on in her apartment and wave from the window. The only suspicious behavior I had exhibited was being black in a block where few—if any—blacks lived.

Afterwards, I found myself wondering whether the outcome would have been as amicable if I had been wearing blue jeans, or had not been carrying my business cards, or had not been in the mood to smile my most congenial smile when the policemen pulled me over.

Whites can easily shrug such encounters off, for it never occurs to them that a white skin might be taken as a sign of criminality. Blacks cannot afford that luxury, not as long as "black continues to mean crime in cities," to quote Moynihan. For the black undercover cop, that equation can literally mean the difference between life and death. For the typical black citizen, it may only mean the inconvenience of being barred from certain stores or stopped on certain streets—along with the unending emotional strain of coping with a society that routinely and capriciously denies one's humanity and individuality. Though the toll may vary from individual to individual, Moynihan's presumption is one that black Americans find pervasive, and one that even intelligence, wit, and Wall Street pinstripes cannot always overcome.

When David Dinkins says that a black millionaire is "a nigger with a million dollars" (apparently a revision of Malcolm X's observation that a black man with a Ph.D. is still a nigger), he is also saying that America's racial legacy makes matters of status and class endlessly complex—and infinitely troubled; that no matter how cultured, how wealthy, and how successful certain blacks become, they will never escape this nation's color-determined caste system.

But that does not stop some people from trying. In the previous chapter, for instance, sociologist Sharon Collins described the attempts of black executives to move out of "black" jobs. It is not that they are trying to escape being black—no more than a black plainclothes officer is trying to escape his race by flashing his shield. What they are trying to escape are the negative consequences of being black and the negative connotations that blackness still carries in American society.

So when Moynihan complains (based on nearly a decade of experience chairing the Senate Subcommittee on Social Security and Family Policy, and seeing maybe three black witnesses who did not have a direct interest in the programs testify about welfare issues) that the black middle class wants nothing to do with the black underclass, he may well be on to something—though not what he thinks. Who comes before congressional committees, after all, is hardly a valid test of who is most interested in a subject. As one lawyer with experience in Washington observed, "Those are not ordinary middle-class white people testifying about any issues either. They are people who are doing it for their living or because they are celebrities." Columnist William Raspberry makes a similar point: "Most of the testimony is not offered by volunteers who say, 'I heard there's a bill being considered on the Hill, I think I'll go down to Washington to testify.'"

The resentment many black professionals feel at being expected to accept responsibility for the underclass is palpable. For instance, Isabel Wilkerson, the *New York Times* Chicago bureau chief, argues that many whites put "entirely too much responsibility and burden on the black middle class for the structural and institutional racism we all inherited. It's not our responsibility. . . . It's the entire country's responsibility. Why should the onus be on . . . the [black] working couple who are just trying to make ends meet, who [themselves] are just one step away from poverty?''

Derrick Bell, in *Faces at the Bottom of the Well*, puts into the mouth of a black cab driver addressing a black professional an even stronger indictment of the black middle class than Moynihan's. "I mean no offense," says the driver, "but the fact is you movin'-on-up black folks hurt us everyday blacks simply by being successful. The white folks see you doing your thing, making money in the high five figures, latching on to all kinds of fancy titles, some of which even have a little authority behind the name, and generally moving on up. They conclude right off that discrimination is over, and that if the rest of us got up off our dead asses, dropped the welfare tit, stopped having illegitimate babies, and found jobs, we would all be just like you.''

Whereas Moynihan is criticizing the black middle class for its indifference, for not getting more actively involved in the problems of the underclass, the cab driver is taking the charge a step further, arguing that black professionals are contributing to the misery of less fortunate blacks simply by being successful.

But even assuming all that to be true (not an assumption many blacks I know would be willing to make), what is it that the black middle class should do to eliminate poverty in black neighborhoods or stop young blacks from shooting each other? Getting black professionals to eschew success—in other words, to become one with the underclass—might eliminate the exasperation some people feel when they see the black middle class held up as an example to the underclass, but it would not improve anyone's condition. Getting black professionals who have no stake in welfare programs more involved with congressional subcommittees such as Moynihan's might conceivably produce more intelligent government initiatives, but there is no logical reason to assume that black accountants or lawyers or doctors—simply because they are black—would have anything more useful to add to the discussion of welfare than academics and social workers who have made research into or amelioration of poverty their life's work. Certainly, black professionals can get involved in any number of ways in the lives of the less fortunate and can make a huge difference in individual cases. That is already happening—on a much larger scale, I suspect, than many people realize. But volunteer work among the disadvantaged is hardly the solution to deep-rooted problems that, as Wilkerson points out, are not the special province and sole preserve of America's black middle class.

Granted, the behavior of some members of the black underclass creates difficulties for practically all blacks, so it is arguably in the interest of middle-class blacks to change that behavior, which bolsters stereotypes that influence attitudes toward the entire race. But even the most superficial and charitable reading of American history reveals that the stereotypes, and the justifications for them, were in place long before anyone imagined a so-called underclass of the type that exists today. Those stereotypes have never needed much confirmation in reality in order to endure.

Hence, one must reserve a high level of skepticism for any argument that would justify stereotypes by pointing to "reality." When Ed Koch contends that "even those who feel deeply about discrimination against blacks . . . feel estranged from the black community," the rational response is not to nod in affirmation but to ask how deeply they can really feel if they would estrange themselves from an entire community because of the actions of a few. When Moynihan insinuates that the efforts of black professionals to advance themselves are futile as long as "black continues to mean crime," one must ask why it is that such a definition can take hold when the vast majority of blacks are demonstrably not criminals, and by what moral, logical, or even economic calculus it makes sense to exhort blacks to achieve as individuals if they are to be judged—and condemned—as a group. When Wilson talks about reducing the black crime rate as the best way to reduce racism, one should ask what purpose is served by a justification of racism—whatever crime statistics show—and whether racism could ever be reduced by accepting assumptions that rationalize stereotypes.

But even if one can put these loaded issues aside, one is left with the question of whether penalizing all blacks for the sins of some blacks makes any sense as a strategy against violent crime. Obviously, keeping blacks out of predominantly white communities, shops, and other institutions would not have much effect on so-called black-on-black crime since it would not isolate blacks from one another. But what effect would it have on crimes against whites? On murder, the most serious crime (and the one for which statistics are the best), it would have relatively little effect since most white homicide victims are killed by other whites. According to FBI statistics, for one-on-one murders tabulated in 1991, 85 percent of white victims were killed by whites. To put it another way, if every black person in America was banished from the country forever, there is no reason to believe that the number of whites getting killed would be much lower than it is.

The fear of black violence cannot be dismissed out of hand. It feeds on images such as those that poured out of Los Angeles during the riots of 1992, when several black men nearly stomped a white truck driver, Reginald Denny, to death. Yet what must be remembered even—indeed, especially—in light of such evil deeds is that incidents in which thugs target someone specifically for racial reasons are not the norm. They also cut both ways. Months after the Denny beating, for instance, a black Brooklyn man on a visit to Florida was kidnapped, drenched in gasoline, and set aflame on the outskirts of Tampa by three white men packing handguns and slinging racial epithets. Indeed, when "hate crimes" occur, it is more often whites who attack blacks (or Asians or Hispanics) than blacks who attack whites.

In 1992, the FBI published its first tabulation ever of "hate crime offenses," covering cases of murder, forcible rape, robbery, aggravated assault, burglary, larceny-theft, motor vehicle theft, arson, simple assault, intimidation, and vandalism, as reported by local law enforcement agencies for 1991. In instances where the perpetrator's race was recorded, 65 percent of assailants were believed to be white, 29 percent to be black, and less than 3 percent to belong to "multiracial" groups. Conversely, of those thought to be targeted because of race, 57 percent were black and 30 percent were white. In other words (calculating from statistics that are admittedly flawed since many localities did not keep good records, and adjusting for the fact that the white population is almost seven times the size of the black population), any particular black person is thirteen times more likely to be the victim of a so-called bias crime than any particular white person.

It is true that a substantial number of blacks commit violent crimes and that the victims are white often enough to generate a reasonable anxiety. But the fact remains that most whites who fall prey to violence are victimized by other whites. And while an examination of what causes people to brutalize members of other racial and ethnic groups is well beyond the scope of this book, it is abundantly clear that no race has a monopoly on senseless violence.

Given that, it is difficult to craft a coherent case for racially discriminatory practices as a strategy for reducing violent crime. At most one might be able to establish the probability that containing blacks in a ghetto, or making forays into predominantly white areas as uncomfortable as possible, would keep violent crime in white communities lower than it would otherwise be. And fearful whites might indeed conclude that the cost (in sales lost, anger generated, and societal values eroded) is worth the extra measure of comfort provided by discrimination. But whether the same objective might be achieved more effectively through more egalitarian methods is a question too seldom asked.

Rather than approach the matter of race and crime analytically, many perfectly intelligent people prefer to take an intellectually lazy path. Instead of analyzing the reality of the black threat, they focus only on the white fear; instead of assessing the soundness of various protective measures, they attempt to justify that fear and the discrimination motivated by it. And thus they foreclose any possibility of constructive dialogue. Clearly, a "solution" that in effect tells law-abiding blacks to abandon their careers and aspirations until they can make black hooligans behave is not a solution at all. It is an excuse for doing nothing, for absolving those whites who wish to wash their hands not only of the problem of crime but of the problem of racial discrimination.

As Senator Bradley points out, crime is an issue that should unite—not divide—along racial lines. But his insight will not be widely accepted as long as fear is used to rationalize discrimination instead of as an impetus to find common ground. Still, unless America is prepared to divide the races even more rigidly than they are divided now, we are ultimately fated to realize that unreasoning rationalizations for white fear will make matters worse for everyone—not just for the blacks those rationalizations seek to burden with responsibility.

For reasons I have explored, law-abiding blacks will never accept full responsibility for black criminals. But even if they did, the problem of crime—and even of violent crime committed by black males—is much too large to be solved by blacks alone. It is all of America's problem, if only because in a mass-media age, and in a culture with deeply rooted racial preconceptions, there is no way to insulate children from the messages the larger society sends. And as long as the dominant message sent to impressionable black boys is that they are expected to turn into savage criminals, nothing will stop substantial numbers of them from doing just that.

chapter six *Affirmative Action and the Dilemma of the "Qualified"*

◆◆◆◆◆◆◆◆◆◆◆◆◆◆◆◆◆◆◆◆◆◆◆◆◆◆◆◆◆◆

W̲HEN THE TALK TURNS TO AFFIRMATIVE ACTION, I often recall a conversation from years ago. A young white man, a Harvard student and the brother of a close friend, happened to be in Washington when the Supreme Court ruled on an affirmative action question. I have long since forgotten the question and the Court's decision, but I remember the young man's reaction.

He was not only troubled but choleric at the very notion that "unqualified minorities" would dare to demand preferential treatment. Why, he wanted to know, couldn't they compete like everyone else? Why should hardworking whites like himself be pushed aside for second-rate affirmative action hires? Why should he be discriminated against in order to accommodate *them?* His tirade went on for quite a while, and he became more indignant by the second as he conjured up one injustice after another.

When the young man paused to catch his breath, I took the occasion to observe that it seemed more than a bit hypocritical of him to rage on about preferential treatment. A person of modest intellect, he had gotten into Harvard largely on the basis of family connections. His first summer internship, with the White House, had been arranged by a family member. His second, with the World Bank, had been similarly arranged. Thanks to his nice internships and Harvard degree, he had been promised a coveted slot in a major company's executive training program. In short, he was already well on his way to a distinguished career—a career made possible by preferential treatment.

My words seemed not to register, and that did not surprise me.

Clearly he had never thought of himself as a beneficiary of special treatment, and no doubt never will. Nor is it likely that either his colleagues or his superiors would be inclined to look down on him as an undeserving incompetent who got ahead on the basis of unfair advantage and was keeping better-qualified people out of work. Yet that assumption is routinely made about black beneficiaries of "affirmative action."

In February 1993, for instance, *Forbes* magazine published an article purporting to demonstrate "how affirmative action slows the economy." The authors referred approvingly to a 1984 poll that "found one in ten white males reporting they had lost a promotion because of quotas." They went on to argue that the poll "was quite possibly accurate. Indeed, it could be an underestimate."

It's impossible from the article to be certain just what poll *Forbes* is citing, but it appears to be a never-published telephone survey by Gordon S. Black Corporation for *USA Today* in which one-tenth of white males answered yes to a much broader question: "Have you yourself ever lost a job *opportunity* or educational *opportunity* at least *partially* as a result of policies and programs aimed at promoting equal opportunity for minorities?" (Emphasis mine.) That, of course, is a very different question from the one *Forbes* reported.

In 1993, *Newsweek* magazine commissioned a national poll that framed the question more narrowly. That poll, interestingly, found even more white males claiming to have been victimized by affirmative action. When asked, "Have you ever been a victim of discrimination or reverse discrimination in getting a promotion?" 15 percent of white males said that they had—the same percentage reporting such discrimination in "getting a job."

Let's assume for the sake of discussion that the *Forbes* figure is correct, and that ten percent of white males do indeed believe that some quota-driven minority person has snatched a position that would otherwise have gone to them. Let's further assume that the ratio holds across occupational categories, so that one out of ten white men in managerial and professional jobs (which, after all, is the group *Forbes* caters to) believes he was unfairly held back by a black or Hispanic colleague's promotion.

Blacks and Hispanics make up 10 percent of the total employees in such jobs, and white males make up 46 percent. So if one out of every ten white males has been held back by a black or Hispanic, that would mean that nearly half of those blacks and Hispanics received promotions they didn't deserve at the expense of white men. (If the *Newsweek* numbers are right, and if we assume that racial and ethnic minorities were the beneficiaries of the "reverse discrimination" suffered by whites, the percentage of minorities who have been unfairly promoted is even higher.) Yet if so many minorities are being promoted ahead of whites, why do black and Hispanic professionals, on average, earn less and hold lower positions than whites? It could be that despite their unfair advantage, minority professionals are so incompetent that whites still manage to get ahead of them on merit. Or it could be that white males who think minorities are zooming ahead of them are way off the mark. *Forbes*, for whatever reason, chose not to consider that possibility. Just as it chose not to consider that the alternative to a system based on "quotas" is not necessarily one based on merit. Or that affirmative action might conceivably result in some competent people getting jobs. Instead, the *Forbes* writers simply assumed such problematic possibilities away. Indeed, like many arguments against affirmative action, their article was not a reasoned analysis at all, but an example of pandering to the anger and anxieties of white males who believe they and their kind are being wronged. And the editors of *Forbes* have plenty of company.

In April 1991, for example, a white Georgetown University law student, Timothy Maguire, set off a tempest in Washington's scholarly and legal communities by questioning the academic quality of blacks admitted to the law school. In an article entitled "Admissions Apartheid," written for a student-controlled paper, Maguire charged that the black law students were in general not as qualified as the whites. The blacks, he said, had lower average scores on the Law School Admissions Tests and lower grade point averages—an allegation based on documents he perused, apparently surreptitiously, while working as a file clerk in the student records office.

The article polarized the campus. On one side were those who demanded that Maguire be expelled for unethical behavior in reading and publishing confidential information. They also raised questions about his mastery of statistics, pointing out that the "random sample" on which he based his conclusions was nothing of the sort, since the files he rifled were only a small selection and included the scores of many applicants who had not been admitted. On the other side were those who saw Maguire as a champion of free speech, a courageous young man who—at risk of public censure—had undertaken to disseminate information that deserved to be debated in a public arena. Maguire apparently saw himself as a victim of leftist ideologues, declaring at one point, according to the *Washington Post*, "It's painful not being politically correct."

In the midst of the ruckus, and after a leak focused attention on Maguire's own academic background, he admitted that his own LSAT scores were below the median for Georgetown students. Interestingly, in light of his charges, coverage of the controversy did not highlight the fact that Maguire got into Georgetown through a special screening program for "low testers," people who would not have been admitted on the basis of their scores but were in effect given extra credit for showing other evidence of promise, dedication, or commitment. In Maguire's case, the fact that he had been a Peace Corps volunteer in Africa weighed heavily in his favor. In short, he was every bit as much a beneficiary of special preference as the black students he scorned.

Shortly after it began, the uproar died down. And despite the protests of the black student organization and others, Maguire was permitted to graduate with his class. Though he was formally reprimanded for violating confidentiality, an agreement worked out by attorneys specifically barred the reprimand from becoming part of his official transcript. Maguire, in short, was allowed to resume a normal life and to put both the controversy and his need for special preference behind him.

Unlike the black students he assailed, who will find their careers haunted by the specter of affirmative action, and who will often be greeted by doubts about their competence whatever their real abilities, Maguire is not likely to suffer because he got into law school on grounds other than academic performance. In other words, he will never be seen as an affirmative action man but simply as a lawyer—entitled to all the recognition conferred by his prestigious degree and all the privileges granted to those presumed to be professionally "qualified."

Why should the presumption of competence differ for black and white graduates of the same school? One answer may be that blacks should be scrutinized more carefully because they are more likely to have met lower admission standards. While that is true in many cases, it is far from true that every black student admitted to a selective school is academically inferior (in any sense of the word) to every white student admitted. Nor is it true, as Maguire's case illustrates, that whites do not receive special treatment in academia. Just as Maguire benefited from a program for "low testers," others benefit from "diversity" policies in East Coast schools that favor residents of Wyoming over those of Connecticut, or from policies that favor relatives of alumni (or children of faculty members, donors, and other influential figures) over those with no family connections. Sometimes universities wish to attract mature students or veterans, or to nurture relationships with certain high schools by admitting their graduates.

One reason for such policies, as virtually any admissions officer will attest, is that prior academic performance is a far from perfect predictor of who will succeed in any specific school, much less who will succeed in life. And that rationale is apparently accepted even by many fervent opponents of affirmative action, since nonracial preferences never seem to elicit anything like the animosity provoked by so-called racial quotas. And even if we grant that many blacks who gain admission with the help of affirmative action are not objectively "qualified," precisely the same can be said about certain children of alumni or about the student who caught the admissions committee's eye because he spent a year on a mission of mercy in Malaysia.

Moreover, determining what it means to be "qualified" is not as easy as it is often made to seem. Ted Miller, who was associate dean of admissions at Georgetown Law at the time of the Maguire imbroglio, points out that many older white professors there—"if they were being honest"—would admit that they could not have met the standards exceeded by the school's typical black student today. As the number of applicants escalated during the 1940s, notes Miller, law schools turned to the LSAT as "an artificial means" to help them sift through applications. And as the numbers continued to increase, the minimum score needed to get into the more exclusive schools (the "qualified threshold") rose. Yet many of those who met the lower standards of the past nonetheless turned out to be distinguished lawyers. Obviously, they were not "unqualified," even if their test results would not win them admission to a prestigious law school today. By the same token, reasons Miller, as long as black students are capable of doing the work, who is to say they are "unqualified"?

Whatever one thinks of Miller's argument, it is unlikely that hostility to affirmative action programs would suddenly vanish if it could be established that "quota" recruits are in fact "qualified." If that were the only issue, programs favoring the children of alumni, say, would provoke the same animus directed at affirmative action. So the primary cause of the hostility must lie elsewhere. And the most logical place to look for it is in American attitudes about race.

In a country largely stuck in a state of denial, any such inquiry is fraught with peril. For one thing, and for any number of reasons (some discussed in chapter 2), Americans have a devil of a time being honest (even with ourselves) when it comes to race. And because determining what our basic attitudes are is so difficult, agreeing on what those attitudes mean may well be impossible.

Not to put too fine a point on it, some people lie—almost reflexively under certain circumstances—about their attitudes regarding race, as public opinion experts have long known. Moreover, the phrasing of the question and the race of the interviewer can make a huge difference in what people say.

In 1989, for instance, pollsters for ABC News and the *Washington Post* asked a random sample of whites, "Do you happen to have a close friend who is black?" When the question was asked by a black, 67 percent of respondents answered yes. When a white asked, the percentage dropped to 57. Conversely, 67 percent of blacks told a black caller they had a close friend who was white, while 79 percent gave the same answer to a white interviewer.

On the question of whether the problems faced by blacks were "brought on by blacks themselves," the variation in responses was even greater. When interviewed by whites, 62 percent of whites said yes. When the same question was asked by blacks, the number dropped to 46 percent. Similarly, when whites were asked by blacks whether it was "very important" for children to attend racially mixed schools, 39 percent said yes, compared to 29 percent who thought so when asked by whites. In all, ABC/*Washington Post* pollsters found that answers varied significantly on more than half of the thirty-three race-related questions in the survey, depending on the race of the interviewer. The disparity might well have been greater if the interviewees could have been absolutely certain of the race of the person on the other end of the telephone line.

Even when the race of the interviewer is not an issue, when people know (or assume) they are talking to someone of their own racial stock, honesty is hardly assured—certainly not in morally charged areas, and especially not when people sense that what they feel is "politically incorrect." Hence, any poll on race must be taken with more than a few grains of salt. When pollsters ask, in one way or another, "Are you a racist?" people know what they are supposed to say. As a consequence, polling has proven to be problematic in political campaigns that pit black and white candidates against each other, because a gap exists between those who say they will vote for a candidate of another race and those who actually will in the privacy of the voting booth. There is no real reason to believe that polls measuring racial attitudes in general are any more accurate. The presumption, instead, should be that they understate the dimensions of racial bias and disharmony. If that presumption is true, the statistics reported below are all the more stunning for what they reveal about the pervasiveness and perdurability of racial stereotypes.

In 1990, 62 percent of whites across America told pollsters for the University of Chicago's National Opinion Research Center (NORC) that they believed blacks were lazier than whites. Fifty-one percent thought blacks likely to be less patriotic. Fifty-three percent said blacks were less intelligent. On every relevant measure of merit or virtue, blacks were judged inferior to whites. What the survey means, in short—despite a widespread belief to the contrary—is that America remains a color-struck society; and there is an abundance of data corroborating that finding.

Two less ambitious polls patterned in part on the National Opinion Research Center's study—in Wisconsin and Los Angeles—yielded results that were strikingly similar. New Yorkers polled in 1992 for the American Jewish Committee rated blacks less intelligent and lazier than the Irish and Italians. Another survey, of 185 employers in the Chicago area, found that those responsible for hiring tended to associate blacks—at least blacks in the central city—with crime, illiteracy, drug use, and a poor work ethic. Many employers had developed strategies (such as recruiting in suburbs and predominantly white schools and advertising in neighborhood and ethnic publications) that allowed them to avoid large numbers of black job applicants. The study, conducted by University of Chicago sociologists Kathryn Neckerman and Joleen Kirschenman, did not focus specifically on firms hiring for professional or executive positions, so its relevance to highly educated blacks is a matter of conjecture; but other research by the same scholars has found that many employers generalize stereotypes of the black underclass to all black applicants.

Not surprisingly, people who see blacks as lazier than whites tend to be among those most strongly opposed to affirmative action. To Tom Smith, director of NORC's general social survey, the reason is obvious: "Negative images lead people to conclude these groups don't deserve this special help." Indeed, it's fairly easy to understand why anyone might have a hard time with the idea that lazy, unintelligent, violence-prone people (whom Americans believe to be disproportionately black and Hispanic) deserve any special consideration at all.

Imagine, for a moment, a society in which there are no different races or ethnic groups, in which everyone sounds and looks essentially the same in terms of color, hair texture, etc. But at birth everyone is branded on the forehead with one of two large letters: either U or W, depending on the letters on their parents' heads. In the case of children of mixed parentage, the child is branded with a U—though a smaller U than children of pure lineage. And if in time that child marries someone wearing the W brand, the mark on their offspring will be smaller yet.

Now imagine that though the two groups are officially equal, a gigantic propaganda campaign is mounted, with the full (if unacknowledged) assistance of the government, to convince everyone that "Unworths" (those with the U brand) are congenitally stupid, lazy, ugly, and unpatriotic, that they make poor neighbors and worse leaders, that in just about every way they are inferior to the "Worths."

Assume that more than 60 percent of the population (including a majority of the Unworths themselves) swallows at least part of the propaganda, so that whenever an Unworth walks into a classroom or office, or tries to buy a home, he or she confronts someone who believes Unworths to be—well, unworthy. Now assume that after an outbreak of violent protests, society decides to eliminate discrimination against Unworths.

The republic passes laws not only guaranteeing access to its institutions but in many cases encouraging preferential treatment of the Unworths. The people who believe in the stereotypes created by the propaganda (in other words, the majority of the population) develop ingenious ways to get around the laws. And they feel virtuous in doing so because they consider any law awarding special privileges to the Unworths patently unfair. Many Unworths, fully accepting the stereotypes of inferiority, shrink from competing with Worths in intellectual or business pursuits. And those Unworths who do manage to get prestigious positions find their right to keep them constantly questioned, and discover that although the number of successful Unworths is very small, the Worths still think there are too many.

Some Unworths become so frustrated by the constant doubting of their competence that they blame the special privileges for their plight—and the Worths strongly encourage them to do so. Indeed, the Worths lavishly praise and promote the books of Unworths who advance such a premise; they put them up for tenured professorships and maybe even name one of them to a special Unworth seat on the highest court of the land. From the perspective of the Worths of the world, given the well-known attributes of Unworths, it is much better to require that individual Unworths prove themselves worthy than to continue to reward so many lazy, unintelligent, and generally unmeritorious people with jobs that belong to the more deserving. And what better allies for the Worths in such an enterprise than articulate Unworths who help make the case.

Now imagine a different scenario. Envision another society where children are branded at birth. But in this society there is only one brand, and it only goes to a very select group: the letter B is impressed on the heads of all children who pass a special test. The test is rather mysterious. No one quite knows how it works, but anyone who passes it is certified to be among the best and the brightest in our imaginary world. Let's assume further that the test was cobbled together by a brilliant prankster who died before he could let the world in on his joke, and that it really doesn't measure anything, that the scores it generates are in fact random. Nonetheless, society accepts the test as perfect, and whoever achieves the requisite score gets to wear the B for life.

Since B-kids are special, society develops them with the utmost care. They are sent to special schools and receive advance placement in the nation's top universities. Even if they prove to be incompetent students, they continue as objects of veneration. Their academic inadequacies are made into virtues. Clearly their true potential cannot be unlocked in the dry and irrelevant world of books, but only in the real world of important affairs. Upon completion of schooling, they are assured countless job offers, many leading directly to the top of the corporate pyramid. Indeed, they find it easy to rise to the top of virtually any field they enter, for everywhere they go they are recognized as the best. And everyone takes that as proof of the meritocracy at work.

Whenever B's walk into a building or a store, they are treated with the greatest respect. Whenever they say something stupid, it is assumed that they were misunderstood, or perhaps were using a vernacular only comprehensible to the elite. And whenever they make decisions with catastrophic results, they are shielded from the consequences—in some cases with multimillion dollar settlements. For everyone understands, that whatever mistakes may have been made, these are extremely deserving individuals.

Their entire lives, in short, are played out as a series of special privileges. And they wear the B as a badge of pride. Very few people resent them. Instead, ordinary folks are delighted to travel in their circles. Even if the high court were to rule that no special treatment be given them, people would defer to them anyway. After all, as everyone can see, they deserve it. They are B's.

The point here is obvious. One cannot honestly and intelligently discuss hostility to preferential treatment without examining attitudes toward those who benefit from the treatment. Well before affirmative action came along, a substantial number of people considered blacks deficient—morally, esthetically, and (especially) intellectually. And if survey findings are any indication, that continues to be the case. It does not mean that *nothing* has changed or that race relations have not improved. It does mean that things have not changed quite as much as many people like to think—and that even in the 1990s, even in the most enlightened of places, black people regularly encounter attitudes that make even the most thick-skinned cringe.

A black woman who had recently graduated from Harvard Law School, for instance, told me she had found her educational experience unsettling, largely because she had not anticipated that she would be treated so differently from whites. She noticed in class that blacks tended to be called on less, but every so often a professor would begin calling on one black student after another—as if the professor had suddenly realized that he was neglecting an important segment of the student body and had resolved to make amends. Whether blacks were called on repeatedly or not at all, she concluded, they were never treated like whites.

A one point, she recalls, a fellow black student went to argue with a professor about a grade. The young man had received a B

minus and thought he deserved something better. Instead of arguing the merits of the case or telling the student how to improve his
work, the professor assured him that there was absolutely nothing
wrong with a B minus. "He would not tell that to a white person,"
the woman said, "but they would tell a black man that a B minus
was a good grade. That he should be satisfied."

Such encounters convinced her that professors expected a very
different level of work from blacks, that in general they felt that
blacks "just don't have the intellectual horsepower." It was "very
rare for a black person to be taken seriously as an intellectual,"
she said. "It was never like the normal thing." The observation
bothered her, for she had not expected to leave Harvard thinking
that. But while her inclination was to assume "that race is not the
explanation for everything," she had seen enough to persuade her
that even at Harvard it explained more than she had supposed.

One could argue that the woman's experience is a perfect example of why affirmative action is ill-advised; that were it not for
an "inclusive" admissions policy, certain black females would not
be at Harvard Law School and therefore would run a substantially
smaller risk of being exposed to people (at least to *Harvard* people) who questioned their "intellectual horsepower." Though the
woman's complaint may indeed illuminate a serious problem with
affirmative action, that does not dispose of the question of underlying attitudes—and what effect they may have on any policy
designed to integrate blacks into institutions historically predis-
posed to doubt their basic abilities.

Ella Bell, of MIT's Sloan School of Management, is among
those who defend affirmative action, but she understands why
others of her background might not. "I think it's very difficult
once we have achieved, and we have good educations, and we
know we're good, we know we have the skills, and we run up
against this brick wall. . . . We've got to have a way to rationalize
that brick wall. And one of the ways I think that we have begun
to rationalize [it] is to say, 'Well, this is because I came in under
affirmative action. If I had come in just like John Doe, I would not
be running into this brick wall. The only reason they can't see my
talent and my skill and all the things that I bring . . . is because I

came in under affirmative action.' . . . What we forget in this dialogue is the whole issue of white racism. And it's very hard to call people on that, because nobody wants to think they're prejudiced. They reject it. They reject it instantly. So we wind up doing this whole rationalization thing, where we're winding up talking about dismantling affirmative action. . . . But affirmative action is a bridge to get us over racist attitudes. . . . It's a necessary mechanism. And it's not about past days . . . from history. This is everyday reality."

"Nobody wants to be perceived as being a victim of racism, or prejudice. It hurts. It hurts deeply," adds Bell, but she does not think that eliminating affirmative action would ease the pain. "No matter what I do, I will still be perceived as a token until you bring in a significant number [of blacks]."

Sharon Collins, the sociologist from the University of Illinois, notes that very few blacks moved into upper management even when affirmative action was in full flower. If that is how blacks fare in a "very supportive environment," she asks, why would anyone presume they would do better if that support were taken away?

One answer, of course, is that it's difficult to conceive of blacks doing much worse under *any* system, that even in the era when affirmative action enjoyed its broadest support, it carried a heavy stigma—one that so undermined the credibility of African-American managers that it virtually guaranteed the results we see today, where less than 1 percent of senior executives at Fortune 500 firms are black.

Without question, many who were hired to fill "minority" slots were never viewed in the same light as other managers. Ulric Haynes, who ran a management recruiting firm in the 1960s (initially specializing in placing minority executives), says the work often left him exasperated. "The most threatening thing that I could do in my minority search activities," he recalls, "was to present a candidate whose qualifications were better than those of the person responsible for recruiting him. They couldn't handle it. . . . If I would present three candidates . . . the predominantly white corporation would invariably select the weakest of the three, not the strongest. . . . They certainly didn't want anybody whose academic preparation was as good as theirs, who spoke English as well as they did, who dressed as well as they did, who moved with grace and ease in their world. . . . They wanted somebody who, by and large, they could sort of feel a little bit sorry for, who would be so happy to have the position that he was entering into [that he] would not cause them any problems in terms of professional advancement."

Not that any client ever said as much to Haynes; he doesn't even think they were cognizant of what they were doing. "This was an unwritten practice. . . . It was so unconscious they weren't even aware of it. But they felt more comfortable with the least qualified than they did with the most qualified." Haynes had not expected to encounter such attitudes, which made the work "discouraging" despite his initial enthusiasm for placing blacks in corporate management.

Only if you assume that (even at some unconscious level) Haynes's corporate clients never expected blacks to shoulder the same responsibilities as white executives does the behavior he describes make sense. For if blacks were not being hired to perform a "white man's job," they would not need a white executive's skills. In fact, possessing such skills (or even obvious competence and excellent credentials) could be a distinct disadvantage—not only because accomplished and confident blacks might demand more power, money, and rank than they could realistically expect, but because it would be much easier to rationalize maintaining the status quo if blacks selected for management were by some set of standards clearly inferior. I cannot vouch for the accuracy of Haynes's recollections; but it's certainly possible that in the 1960s, when black executives were being hired almost exclusively (in truth, if not in title) for "black" jobs, employers gravitated toward those without the savvy, standing, or inclination to advance or rock the boat.

Such strange behavior can be seen less as the fault of white employers than as the natural result of attitudes that place more emphasis on getting minorities into visible jobs than on making the best use of all available talent. In that light, such practices become a powerful argument against any kind of racial preference—especially in the 1990s, when companies can no longer afford to keep people just for show. If affirmative action creates so many problems—even for those it was designed to benefit—could a society that eschewed it conceivably do any worse?

Stephen Carter, author of *Reflections of an Affirmative Action Baby*, argues that people of color might be much better served by the free market than by any explicit scheme of racial preferences. "Left to itself, the market isn't racist at all," he writes, "and if highly qualified minority scholars or lawyers or doctors are a more valuable commodity than white ones, a free market will naturally bid up their price. That is what markets do (at least in the absence of regulation) when valuable commodities are in short supply; outstanding professionals who are members of desirable minority groups are expensive for the same reason that gold or diamonds are expensive. And that is evidently the result that the market currently produces, at least at the top end."

How is one to square Carter's view with Haynes's lament that the top ranks of Fortune 500 companies remain all but closed to African Americans, and that even large companies not on the Fortune 500 list have locked the CEO's office to blacks (except a conspicuous few, such as the late Reginald Lewis, who bought TLC Beatrice International Holdings in 1987, and Richard Parsons, who was named chief executive officer of Dime Savings Bank in 1990). "Certainly, given the fact that the first wave of minority group executives entered Fortune 500 companies in the late 1960s, certainly by now one would have made it, at least to be one of the top three executives in a Fortune 500 company," says Haynes. "I can't think of anyone who's made it to the top. By the law of averages, one of us, even if we didn't stay there, should have gotten to be chief financial officer."

One reason Haynes and Carter disagree is that they are looking at different markets. The market for law partners or university faculty members is considerably larger than the market for Fortune 500 CEOs. To put it another way, a law firm with one hundred partners or a university with two hundred faculty slots might easily see how they could profit by naming blacks to a few of those posts. A firm with only one CEO, however, is likely to view things differently. In my profession, there is considerable evidence of Carter's market theory in action. It is generally accepted among newspaper executives that a big-city daily needs at least some minority journalists in order to do an adequate job. As a result, the bidding for black, Hispanic, and Asian reporters considered top-notch can sometimes get furious. A few years ago, Ben Bradlee, then editor of the *Washington Post,* became so annoyed that the *New York Times* was trying to recruit his best black reporters that he wrote a note to the *Times* editor volunteering to send him a list of them. Despite the intense competition for black reporters, however, the top tier of newspaper management remains overwhelmingly white. None of the nation's biggest and most prestigious papers (or the three major news magazines) has installed an African American as its principal editor.

There are reasons for the scarcity of blacks at the top, some having to do with race and some not, but anyone who sees newspapers and other large organizations as nothing more than economic units in a gigantic market is bound to miss many of them. Newspapers in the real world are not elegant abstractions full of people with perfect knowledge and perfect access, driven purely by a desire to maximize profit. They are much more (for lack of a better word) *human* than that.

Even economists these days don't hew to the view that the "market" always knows what is best. Economist Herbert Stein, for instance, tells the story of two men, one an economist and one not, who were out for a stroll when the noneconomist stopped dead in his tracks and exclaimed, "Look, there's a $20 bill lying on the sidewalk!" The economist responded, "No, there can't be. If there had been, it would already have been picked up."

People don't always know where the money lies in life, and as a result they don't always make decisions that maximize their wealth, even if that is their intention. And often that is *not* their intention. Human beings, after all, are not bloodless calculators. They often act in romantic, altruistic, or merely mysterious ways. The same sort of emotional attachment that can lead a father to try to fulfill his dreams through his son, or a mother to sacrifice

everything, including life itself, for the welfare of her family, operate—though generally in much milder ways—in the work environment, which is as much a social organization as an economic one.
So decisions get made, and people get accepted (and rapidly promoted), for reasons that have nothing to do in a direct way with
profit maximization. Perhaps a corporate officer sees a younger
version of himself in the appearance and style of a certain young
man. Or maybe a subordinate shares a passion for an exotic sport,
or for a particular kind of after-hours entertainment. And even for
competent people, especially blacks, such social bonding can present a problem. As Edward Jones observes: "The kinds of social
relationships, the kinds of acceptance by others [needed to ad-
vance], are not within your control. You can't make somebody
love you or root for you."

Moreover, however much corporate mandarins like to think of
themselves as risk-seeking entrepreneurs, most senior executives
of established firms avoid risk whenever they can—not only looking out for their own economic welfare by negotiating compensation packages that never go down, regardless of their performance, but by rejecting any personnel move that seems a radical
departure from the norm. And in many conservative corporate
cultures, moving a black person into a sensitive job would be seen
as an unacceptable risk, irrespective of that person's abilities. As
the *New York Times* executive in chapter 3 insinuated in explaining his hesitation to promote a certain black man, the very fact
that a black had never previously held the post constituted part of
the argument as to why one should not. Only after the "first
black" managed to succeed would that particular barrier be
removed.

The hesitation to move blacks along may have nothing to do
with personal prejudice, but with a perception that putting a black
person in a visible slot might have economic consequences—a
perception that makes sense if one assumes (whatever the reality)
that some segments of the market or some players who influence
the market might be disturbed to see a black person in a job where
only whites are normally seen. In assessing the comfort level of
whites with very visible blacks, most executives have only assump-

tions to guide them, and those assumptions tend to be conservative, often to the point of rigidity. Until very recently, for instance, one big-city paper had an explicit policy against running more than one minority op-ed columnist a day, regardless of the columns' subject matter, perspectives, or quality. The assumption apparently was that while whites were comfortable with one non-white pictured in the commentary section of the newspaper, they would not be comfortable with more. So the editor had taken it upon himself to protect his readers from encountering too many minority writers.

Even if there were no explicit racial criteria at work, the market model would have obvious limits. Assuming that a market existed for "good people" and that it was to the economic advantage of the firm to make sure that such people were allowed, relative to others in the organization, to go as far as their abilities could take them, how would the organization recognize the best talent? To many, the answer seems obvious. That is exactly what they assume corporations are already doing. Isn't it self-evident that simply out of economic self-interest, a firm would do everything within its power to ensure that the best people were in the most appropriate jobs? Yet as discussed in chapter 4, many people (perhaps most) end up in jobs for reasons that seem to have little to do with merit. Edward Irons and Gilbert Moore, in their research on black bankers, were surprised to find that "virtually 100 percent of the interviewees indicated that the most important criterion for promotion was 'who you know,' or 'being plugged into the political system.'" Technical competence, in their eyes, counted for little.

Perhaps we can dismiss the bankers interviewed by Irons and Moore as extremists of some sort, but it's much more difficult to dismiss the mountain of academic studies, personal narratives, and anecdotal evidence that reveals the workplace as a social institution run largely on the basis of favoritism, stereotypes, and unexamined (often incorrect) suppositions. While affirmative action may have aggravated the problem, for all we know it has not. It may just be that *that is the way the workplace works*—or at least the way it has worked so far.

Hence, one is not quite sure what to make of Stephen Carter's declaration of war on racial preferences, or of the fact that he apparently expects an army of black professionals to join his crusade. The time will come, he speculates, when "we, the professionals who are people of color, decide to say that we have had enough—enough of stereotyping, enough of different standards, enough of the best-black syndrome." But Carter's stirring rhetoric obscures an important question. If in fact affirmative action does not account for all the problems he so eloquently pinpoints, then what, upon reflection, should be the response? If stereotyping, double standards, and professional ceilings exist quite independently of formal racial preference programs, how eager should we be to join the movement to abolish affirmative action? And if we assume that people in general, and employers in particular, tend to be marginally competent in assessing merit and potential irrespective of race, what are we to think of Carter's desire "to show the world that we who are black are not so marked by our history of racist oppression that we are incapable of intellectual achievement on the same terms as anybody else."

The problem he addresses is a real one. Yet the presumption of lesser competence is a cross borne not only by blacks who were "affirmative action hires," but at one time or another by many blacks who were not; by most blacks, in fact, who have ever found themselves working for a major American institution. That presumption is difficult, if not impossible, to overcome, which raises the obvious question of exactly what proof it would take to "show the world" that blacks are capable of real intellectual achievement.

I suspect that those inclined to believe in the possibility of genuine black achievement will accept that proposition even in the absence of absolute proof; or will note that blacks throughout history have already accomplished so much that yet another demonstration is unnecessary; or will point out that blacks, as Americans, deserve to be treated as individuals and equals without having to prove their worth first. On the other hand, those not inclined to believe that blacks are capable of any real intellectual achievement will reject "proof" of it with one of several responses. They may praise the black person who finally "shows" them as an "exception," and therefore not really black. Or they may claim that whatever feat of genius a black person performs, it is a simple intellectual parlor trick that demonstrates nothing at all. Or they may accept the proffered proof but then demand that blacks pass yet another test, that black professionals, for instance, make the black crime rate equal the white crime rate before they presume the right to be treated as equals. Common sense, in short, dictates that there is no such thing as proving such a proposition to a world unwilling to believe it, and no need to prove it to a world disposed to accept it.

To expect that abolishing affirmative action would make black intellectual capability easier to prove strikes me as more than a little naive. Just as to argue, as Carter does, that "affirmative action has done nothing at all for the true victims of racism" strikes me as myopic. Putting aside the question of whether affirmative action has truly benefited most members of any class, who exactly are these "true victims of racism"? Presumably, in Carter's mind, they are the poor souls who populate the underclass. Yet if you believe the volumes of evidence that show racial problems and racial stereotypes percolating through every level of American society, you could argue that just about every American, whatever his or her race, is a true victim of racism.

For all my problems with Carter's analysis, I believe he has a compelling point: that affirmative action or racial preference programs will never bring blacks into parity with whites. And I'm sure that others who might disagree with much of what he says would not disagree with him on that. Roosevelt Thomas, founder of the American Institute for Managing Diversity, comes to a similar conclusion about affirmative action from a different set of premises. "Sooner or later, affirmative action will die a natural death. Its achievements have been stupendous, but if we look at the premises that underlie it, we find assumptions and priorities that look increasingly shopworn," he wrote in 1990 in the *Harvard Business Review*.

I will return to Thomas later. Suffice it to say here that like many black professionals, I find myself profoundly ambivalent on the question of affirmative action. I don't believe that it works very well, nor that it can be made to satisfy much of anyone. Moreover, I believe that programs based on racial preferences are inherently riddled with the taint and the reality of unfairness. I don't, however, believe that such programs belong on any list of the most odious things to have befallen America. And I certainly don't believe—despite the anguished cries of untold numbers of white men—that such programs have had much to do with the inability of any but a handful of whites to get hired or promoted. I believe, rather, that affirmative action has been made the scapegoat for a host of problems that many Americans simply don't wish to face up to; and that while a huge and largely phony public debate has raged over whether affirmative action is good or bad, the reality is much more nuanced and complex. In recent days, that debate has sometimes pitted so-called black conservatives against so-called black liberals. Yet I doubt that if pressed to the wall, the two sides would find themselves in much disagreement—at least over the essential bankruptcy of affirmative action as a policy to foster workplace equality. Where their more fundamental disagreement lies is in their assessment of the virtues of whites. Would whites treat everyone more equally if affirmative action wasn't gumming up the works? Without the millstone of affirmative action, would corporations and other large organizations be more capable of judging people on performance, potential, and merit rather than on preconceptions and office politics? Would acceptance as full members of the American family come easier if the prod were taken away? One side, in effect, says yes, and the other says no.

These are not questions of fact, for the future, by definition, is unknown. They are essentially questions of faith—of whether one believes in the ability and willingness of those whites who still control the majority of important institutions in America to do what they have not done thus far: ensure that no group is systematically penalized as a consequence of color.

In March 1961, when John F. Kennedy signed Executive Order 10925, which created the President's Committee on Equal Employment Opportunity and brought the phrase affirmative action into common usage, he apparently had little more than that in mind: ''The contractor will not discriminate against any employee or applicant for employment because of race, creed, color or national origin . . . [and] will take affirmative action to ensure that applicants are employed, and that employees are treated during employment, without regard to their race, creed, color, or national origin.'' The difficulty companies had in carrying out that simple injunction is a story much too tangled and complicated even to begin to detail here; but the fact that they in large measure did not carry it out explains both why we are still debating affirmative action more than three decades later and why so many blacks are reluctant to take a leap of faith.

Imagine a brown, unpopular child who wants more than anything to be a runner. His classmates refuse to let him run with them, or even to practice on *their* track. When he dares to go near it, they taunt him, and then they push him away. A kindly official, noticing the harassment, decides to give the boy a break. He declares that even if the other children will not let the brown kid practice with them, they must let him run in every scheduled public race. Moreover, since the boy is at a disadvantage because he has not been allowed to practice with them, the official orders all the other boys to give him a five-yard head start.

As the first race approaches, the boy is both apprehensive and elated. He is unsure of his own abilities but delighted that he will finally have a chance to show all the other kids what he can do, and he is comforted by the thought that once he does they will finally accept him as a peer. On the day of the race, however, an unexpected thing happens. Even before he starts to run, the crowd pelts him with garbage and stones. When the race begins, he stumbles and the other kids catch up with him. Some pass him with looks of concern and sympathy, others pass with looks of scorn, and a few even elbow him or kick him as they scamper on their way.

The experience repeats itself race after race; and as the child struggles to understand why he is being treated so, he learns that the people in the crowd suffer from a strange affliction, that though they can see him well enough to abuse him, no one up there can really see what he is going through. Those in the stands can see, at most, a fraction of the objects that fly his way; and those who are hurling them can't understand their force. He learns that many of the onlookers pity him, that some refuse to throw stones and even whisper words of encouragement, but that most deeply resent the fact that the other kids had to let him into the race, and that they resent his five-yard head start even more.

Though the official has given a very public and heartfelt explanation for the special treatment, loudmouths in the bleachers focus increasingly on the unfairness of the brown kid's head start. Why is it necessary? If he must run, why can't he start with the other kids? Could he be genetically inferior? If so, why is he running at all? And why in the blazes can't he ever win even with a head start? Could he have a psychological problem? Is he lazy? Is he stupid? Is something in his culture keeping him from keeping up?

Soon the questions have reached such a pitch that the mere sight of the kid on the track is enough to whip the crowd into a frenzy. The child, as he comes to understand the anger of the mob, realizes that even with a five-yard head start, he will never win. And he doesn't know whether he should ask for a bigger lead, give up the one he has, or simply abandon the race.

chapter seven *Young People, Old Ideas*

◆◆◆◆◆◆◆◆◆◆◆◆◆◆◆◆◆◆◆◆◆◆◆◆◆◆◆◆

N̲O SANE PARENT WISHES TO EXPOSE A CHILD to hurtful insults and gratuitous pain. Yet for African-American parents, the normal impulse to nurture and protect their children can land them on the horns of a dilemma: whether to expose the children to racial prejudice so they will be better able to fight it, or to prepare them for a world in which race is not an issue—which is to say, for a world that may not exist. Even though the parents may have spent all their lives wrestling with the demons of race, there are no obvious answers. In a quickly changing society, where the racial landscape is constantly shifting, their own experience negotiating America's often treacherous racial byways may be of little use as a guide.

Some sense of the dilemma can be derived from the confusion of the lawyer profiled in chapter 1, who pondered how to educate children "with the hope they will be given a fair shot" while simultaneously equipping them with enough psychological armor to survive the "street fight" and the crippling effect of racial bias. Or from the regret of Hofstra business school dean Ulric Haynes at not having prepared his children, "in all the years that we lived overseas, to deal with the climate of racism that they are encountering right now."

"Children are a problem in this period," agrees former United Nations ambassador Donald McHenry. "They are a problem in terms of preparation and a problem socially. And I see this not only with my own children but with others." He knows parents, for instance, who attended private schools and Ivy League universities, but who—wishing to spare their children unpleasant experiences or give them a more solid grounding in black culture or a deeper sense of what it means to be black—send them to Howard University, Spelman College, or other historically black institutions. And he has personally experienced the challenge of raising children in an area where there are virtually no other African Americans.

"You are the one black family, or one of two, or whatever. Your children have . . . either lived in the suburbs or gone to small private schools and so forth. They in one sense grow up having competed [against whites] every day of their lives. And that is not a problem. What is a problem for them is the social problem of isolation. Some of them adjust to it much better than others. . . . They either have to have a healthy attitude or they have a rude awakening to the larger society, a society which is larger than their little cocoon.

"You try to bring them up with a healthy attitude, to know they are not as isolated as their isolation would lead them to believe. You don't succeed all the time. There is, some time in their experience, that rude awakening, that one incident that I saw all the time when I was a kid, but from which they, in a sense, have been sheltered. . . . Some young people adjust. Some do not. . . . I think it depends on how children are brought up, how they are exposed. What kinds of discussions go on around the family table. What you do to make sure that they have a full appreciation of the world."

Ulric Haynes long wrestled with one of the central conundrums of raising black middle-class children: how to give them a good education, spare them soul-wounding experiences, and also expose them to the larger world. "When my children became of school age, in this country," says Haynes, "I wanted them to be in an educational environment that offered quality education as well as cultural diversity. I couldn't find it in any public school in any of the communities in which I lived. . . . The paradox is that in order to find the socioeconomic and the ethnic diversity and the quality education for my children, I had to send them to private schools. The most prestigious private schools in the country are making an effort to build into the school population that kind of diversity.''

McHenry says that he has seen an intriguing change in some of his friends, people who earlier in their lives refused to attribute any of their problems to race—''That wasn't a barrier . . . they recognized''—but who have come to believe that the barrier is there after all and are ''quite bitter about it—the glass ceiling.'' And at least in some instances, the shift in perspective seems directly related to what is happening with their children. ''They see their children as rather isolated, in part because of the kinds of opportunities they [the parents] have had and where they have lived. They don't have the kinds of social contacts and so forth they might have had.'' McHenry confesses uncertainty as to the extent of the phenomenon he describes: ''That may be a particular age group. And it may be a particularly privileged group. It may not be John Q. Run-of-the-mill who now considers himself middle class.''

Certainly, as McHenry suggests, most black parents—even those who belong to the middle class—are in no position to send their children to expensive private schools and sequester them in suburbia. Nor, for that matter, do many parents of any color spend much time worrying that their exclusion from private clubs might wreak havoc with their children's future. But even blacks of relatively modest means find the choices for their children anything but clear. For though everyone knows that times are changing, most also know (or think they do) that the world their children will inherit will remain a racially troubled place. And most do not have to look beyond their own experience to find support for that supposition.

Terri Dickerson-Jones, who lives in a predominantly white suburban community in Virginia, remembers the misery she endured as a child when Catholic schools were integrated in her home state of Louisiana. Her parents had never talked to her much about racial prejudice, so when she went to her first-grade class and some white children called her and other blacks ''niggers,'' she was dumbfounded: ''It was like a stunning discovery to me that I was *different*.'' Her own son, she decided, could do without such surprises, so she made a point of teaching him about bigotry. And when a white female schoolmate invited him home only to rescind the invitation the following day, the boy took the rejection in stride. The girl's mom, he explained, was "prejudiced," so he would not be going to her home after all. He was not particularly shocked by the rejection, said Dickerson-Jones, though "I suppose under different circumstances he might have been." But as it was, he mostly felt sorry for his young friend, whose mother was apparently so disagreeable.

Mary Curtis, a *New York Times* editor who lives in a largely white suburb, has also wrestled with how best to prepare her son for a racially polarized world. She takes comfort and pride in the fact that her ten-year-old, whose father is white, has escaped the most common stereotype: "At school, he's known as the smart kid, not the black kid." But she refuses to be Pollyannaish. "We don't fool ourselves into thinking that everyone's accepted him. . . . We don't want, because we're being naive, to have him hurt some day." So she teaches him about prejudice, turning his television-news-inspired questions about Thurgood Marshall and Rodney King into mini-lessons on black history. And she lets him know that black males stopped by the police have to be especially careful, that "the cop is your friend *sometimes*." Like McHenry, she also worries about the hazards of racial isolation, and she insists that some of her son's activities be in settings where nonwhites are not in the minority (such as his predominantly black and Hispanic martial arts class); for she has seen too many black children raised in suburbia who, like legions of young whites, harbor fearful and terrible stereotypes of inner-city blacks.

Though she is generally hopeful about race relations ("You always want to think things are going to be better for your child"), she also fears trouble down the line. The country is becoming more and more nonwhite, she says, "and many whites have a problem with that." She sees a growth in racial resentments and a "digging in" among certain whites as harbingers of an imminent deterioration in an already ugly racial climate. "The same people who are patting him on the back, if they ever feel they're in competition with him, those [racial] sentiments will come out.

They will belittle his achievements because it makes them feel better . . . and even if he knows what it is, it will still hurt him."

Indeed, no matter how well prepared people seem to be, bigotry can sting. A young woman who graduated from Harvard Law School in her twenties and has won more than her share of honors says she feels ambushed whenever she hears a cutting racial remark. "Oddly, I still don't expect it." Every time she is treated badly because of race, she finds the experience nearly as painful as being hit with prejudice for the first time. That is a cross she supposes she will always have to bear; for race is "the one thing you can't do anything about."

But more confusing than outright bigotry have been situations where no hostility was evident and no insult was intended. At one law firm, for instance, though no one told her they assumed she was incompetent, she sensed from the way the partners behaved that they just didn't expect much from her. So when her performance exceeded their expectations, she was uncomfortable with their praise. It felt patronizing, as if they were congratulating her for being capable of serious thought.

When she started work at another law firm with black partners, her unease vanished. Having found someone who could help guide her through the firm, she felt less need to search for hidden meanings in casual comments and less pressure to act as an ambassador for her race. The extent to which she relaxed surprised her. Though she had known all along that she was weary "of being the first and the only," she was surprised how much difference the presence of other blacks could make: "I guess I never realized when I was the only one how lonely I was."

This young lawyer, like many of her generation who have gone to the best schools and been welcomed into the most elite sanctums, doesn't know whether her color will severely limit her options in life, but she is apprehensive. "I assume that race is not the explanation for everything. . . . We too often turn to race as the only explanation." Yet she worries about the future, about confronting "an invisible hurdle, an invisible bar," as she puts it. "In some way, I think the worst part is yet to come."

A similar sense of foreboding haunts Stephanie Gilliam, another woman from a privileged background, also in her twenties, also trying to figure out her generation's racial destination. The daughter of Sam Gilliam, a well-known Washington artist, and Dorothy Gilliam, a columnist for the *Washington Post*, she knows firsthand what it means to emerge into the society beyond what McHenry calls the "little cocoon." Throughout childhood she attended small, very liberal, and overwhelmingly white private schools. Yet she never felt that she was being treated differently from her white classmates. She would hear Jewish jokes and sometimes black jokes, but she never sensed that the jokes were directed at her. "I did not fit the stereotype of what they expected a black to be," she recalls. But when she emerged from the private school sanctuary, she found herself in a very unfamiliar place— one that was simultaneously appealing and disappointing.

At Brown University, unlike in grade school or high school, the majority of Gilliam's friends were black. She enjoyed the new sense of fellowship and gained unexpected insight into a largely unexplored world. She learned, for instance, about complexion-based discrimination among African Americans. And she learned, more significantly, that the nurturing private environment of childhood had left her with a very incomplete view of American racial attitudes. That lesson was driven home even more forcefully after she graduated from Brown and returned to Washington to pursue a degree in architecture at Catholic University. At her part-time job in a Georgetown restaurant, she found that people assumed she was either from Howard University or the predominantly black University of the District of Columbia. And she found that many people had false preconceived notions of what she, a black woman, should be.

When I talked with her in 1992, she was sorting out her reactions. "I don't really know if I'm angry," she said. "I think it [racial prejudice] is something I've accepted. . . . I think it makes me sad. I think I expected I was growing up in a world where we'd all be able to live together." Reality, she was discovering, was quite different. "It's almost as if we've given up trying to live together." So she tried to shut out the disharmony and "do my own thing."

She is acutely aware that her experience is different from that of most Americans, black or white—and also different from what her parents had expected it to be. They had assumed, she says, that they were giving her the best of both worlds, that she would get a high-quality liberal education in mainly white schools but be integrated into the wider society through living in a very racially mixed neighborhood. As a result she would learn to get along with people of all kinds. The problem was that "the experiment didn't work." Though she returned each day to a community of ethnic minorities, the black neighborhood kids never fully accepted her; she was from a different school, and in many respects from a different universe. And she is still not completely sure where she belongs: "I feel like I'm very much in the middle."

Leslie Estes, another young black middle-class woman who lives in the Washington area, feels far less conflicted than Gilliam, in part because she has always been aware that racial harmony is not an especially natural state. Estes, who was raised in Pough-keepsie, New York, remembers being in a Lutheran day care center at the age of four and realizing that a white girl, repulsed by her color, was refusing to sit next to her. "More than anything, I remember that." She also recalls struggling to understand why her grandfather's hatred of white people seemed to increase with his age, and why in grade school all the black kids were stuck in the "problem child class." In her own case, the tracking didn't last; her mother, a teacher, insisted that she be grouped with the "normal" children.

Estes attended Hampton University, a historically black institu-tion, because she didn't want the pressure of coping with white expectations—which she assumed would largely be expectations of failure. She agrees that it would be great if everyone were judged on merit but has concluded, "It's not like that. It's never been like that. It's never going to be like that." For evidence she need only look at her boyfriend, who is also black and who is routinely stopped by the police when visiting her suburban Vir-ginia community. "Just listening to the things he goes through makes me angry," she says, noting that similar indignities are rarely visited on young white men.

Along the spectrum of reactions to race-related experiences, Estes and Gilliam have ended up in quite different spots: one with hope that race relations will get significantly better, the other with certainty that they will not. Their attitudes, ranging from optimism to despair, mirror those held by young people of all races across America.

In 1992, Peter D. Hart Research Associates polled a cross-section of Americans ages fifteen through twenty-four for People for the American Way and glumly concluded that "racial divisions are taking root among a new generation." But the researchers also hit a much more upbeat note: "These young people are beginning life with high ideals, more inclined . . . to hope than to hate." Young Americans, "if summoned to do so, will support the principle of racial fairness and mutual respect," they predicted.

The reason for this mixed message is apparent from their findings. Seventy-one percent of respondents reported having at least one "close personal friendship" with a member of another race, yet 53 percent of whites (and 62 percent of blacks) thought most whites felt uneasy dealing with blacks, and 54 percent of whites (and 52 percent of blacks) thought blacks were generally uncomfortable with whites. While the vast majority of respondents said racial integration was worthwhile, 56 percent of whites thought they would "not be safe going into most black neighborhoods," and 41 percent of blacks felt the same way about white neighborhoods. While 60 percent of young whites thought race relations were improving, half of the young blacks thought they were getting worse.

The majority of whites (81 percent) agreed that racial and ethnic minorities still faced "a lot of discrimination in our society," but many apparently felt that was more than offset by affirmative action. For instance, when asked to choose among three alternatives—whether blacks "are receiving too many special advantages, are receiving fair treatment, or are being discriminated against"—48 percent said blacks were getting "too many" advantages, 47 percent said they were being treated fairly, and only 4 percent deemed them victims of discrimination. At another point, 55 percent of whites accepted the view that "blacks have caused many of their own problems, but make excuses by blaming them on discrimination instead.''

Not surprisingly, then, a majority (51 percent) of young whites opposed ''special consideration'' for minority college applicants, and even more (65 percent) opposed ''special consideration to minority job applicants.'' When the phrase ''special preferences'' was substituted for ''special consideration,'' white opposition went even higher. Even most blacks, while supporting ''special consideration,'' rejected the idea of ''special preferences'' for minority job seekers. And more blacks than whites (82 to 76 percent) thought it would ''help a lot'' in dealing with racial problems if society could ''get people to take more responsibility for themselves, rather than blaming others for their problems.''

Given this welter of incongruous and even contradictory perceptions, it is hardly surprisingly that so many young people are confused. Yet within the welter lies a consistent message. Young whites are saying, in effect, that they are different from their counterparts of the 1940s and 1950s, who by and large accepted discrimination as the natural order. This ''next generation'' believes discrimination to be evil and integration to be good—at least in most things, most of the time. Yet like their parents, many young whites wonder whether the pendulum has swung too far, whether they are being asked to pay too high a price for racial injustices that are really not all *that* unjust, and that they certainly did not cause. So even as they idealize an abstract fairness, they also bristle with resentment at what they perceive as a racial preference system that gives blacks more than their due at the expense of whites, and that undermines the essential concept of a just society by rewarding blacks who refuse to help themselves.

Young blacks are every bit as unhappy as young whites about perceived social injustice. The big difference, of course, is that they see themselves as much more likely than whites to be victimized by it; a substantial number, in fact, believe they already have been. As a result, many are either angered or bewildered by the unwillingness or inability of their white contemporaries to see the world from their point of view. And even though they may have close white friends, the majority have little expectation that relationships with whites will be anything other than awkward, by and large. Such views are based, at least to some degree, on their own experiences—experiences that have led them to be suspicious or frankly mistrustful of young whites' commitment to racial equality. For even though they know that in many respects their lives are much better than those of their parents and grandparents, and that opportunities their forebears could only dream about may be handed to them on a platter, they also fear that America's best years may well be in the past, and that they, much more so than their young white friends, will be penalized for their country's problems. Young people of all races, in short, see a world whose racial crosscurrents and interracial possibilities are murkier than ever, a world where amity flourishes alongside race-based resentment.

Perhaps it was this resentment that drove Georgetown University's Timothy Maguire to expose what he considered the inferior qualifications of black law students, and motivated a fraternity at Rider College in New Jersey, in early 1993, to stage "Dress Like a Nigger Night," during which white pledges were required to wear baggy clothing and X's on their foreheads while scrubbing out the fraternity house. Perhaps analogous racially based grievances have inspired black student groups across the country to invite speakers to spew anti-white (particularly anti-Jewish) invective as they spell out sweeping indictments of whites for virtually everything bad that has ever happened to blacks.

Resentment, of course, does not materialize out of nowhere. For young whites, the sources are multiple: an economy that cannot ensure them employment, affirmative action programs that slap them in the face, and a host of other signs, imagined and real—all exploited by demagogues of racial unrest—telling them that for all the pandering to minorities, whites are really the group that is being wronged. For young blacks, the list of grievances is at least as long. They are more concerned about the economy than whites, for they know (or suspect) that even for college graduates, the black unemployment rate typically runs twice that for whites. And they have experienced—or know people who have—the rage and utter helplessness of being singled out solely for the color of their skin and being treated like dirt.

Many blacks, young and old alike, were forced anew to confront those feelings in September 1992, when an administrator at State University of New York's College at Oneonta released the names of all black male students to police. The police were seeking a young black man who had tried to rape a seventy-seven-year-old white woman. She had managed not only to fend the assailant off but to cut him on the arm with the knife he was brandishing. So the police went in search of a young black man with cuts on his arm—a task they presumed the university's list would simplify. There was nothing subtle about their methods; they tracked down the male black students, one by one, demanded to see their arms, and made them account for their whereabouts at the time of the crime. No student was charged, and Oneonta officials were initially inclined to treat the incident as nothing more than an isolated instance of overzealousness. Blacks on campus, however, saw it as symptomatic of something deeper, as a refusal to see past the color of their skin and a reminder of how fragile was their status in the predominantly white town. A black college administrator bluntly told a *New York Times* reporter, "It was a chance to humiliate 'niggers.' "

The same bitterness and sense of persecution felt by many blacks in Oneonta is felt on numerous other college campuses. And it collides constantly with white resentments at those same institutions. With such feelings running so deep (but so quick to rise to the surface) and commingling with a generally strong desire for racial harmony, it's easy to understand why young people are torn.

Despite all the confusion and ambivalence, there is a fair consensus that the state of race relations is bad. Fifty percent of young people think so, according to the above-mentioned poll, though even on that question there is a racial gulf: blacks are more likely than whites (57 to 48 percent) to say that race relations in the United States are generally bad. And while most whites think they are getting better (60 percent, compared to 30 percent who think they are getting worse), blacks are markedly more pessimistic.

Forty-three percent think things are improving, while 46 percent believe they are in decline.

The perceptual gulf, the contradictory findings, the flowering of resentments, the frequency of racial incidents—all lead toward an inescapable conclusion: racial discord will be with us for a long, long time. This "next generation," for all its idealism, openmindedness, and willingness to embrace equality and racial integration, is not even close to mastering the art of how to get along.

Once upon a time, of course, many thought that racial division would soon be a thing of the past, that the next generation, or perhaps the one after that, would achieve harmony where their parents could not. Martin Luther King's may have been the most famous 1960s dream, but he was not dreaming alone. Yet as today's young people come of age, many one time idealists are beginning to think that such dreams are rooted in little more than fantasy.

One woman I know, the mother of several adoptive sons whose early childhood was spent with negligent parents, says she has seen through the eyes of her children how certain racial assumptions are formed. Having spent a substantial amount of time in the family-court and child-welfare system, where their destiny has been decided largely by whites, the children have concluded that whites are the people in charge and that blacks are the ill-treated and the unwanted. They have learned, as a result, to loathe themselves—and especially the color of their skin. The adoptive parents, both well-educated professionals, were so alarmed to uncover such self-hatred that they devised games that allow the children to declare themselves smart, talented, and beautiful.

In a nation where blacks continue to be perceived in largely unfavorable ways, those children will have an extremely difficult struggle merely coming to terms with who—and what—they are. Even as their parents try to teach them self-love, other parents will teach their children to stereotype them.

Several years ago, I happened to be in the home of a woman of Mexican-American extraction who had a charming and precocious daughter. In the course of the evening it came to light that the mother had schooled her child in what could make a neighborhood "bad." Whatever precise lesson the mother had been trying to teach, the youngster had grasped what seemed to be the essential fact: that a neighborhood was bad if it happened to be black.

That the young girl already had such a racially tinted picture of reality seemed to me almost tragic. I left that evening with a sense of sadness akin to what I had felt some months before, when a New York taxi driver, a Korean immigrant, responded to my questioning the fare by flooring the accelerator once I was out of his cab and shouting something about "niggers." From his thick accent and his obvious difficulty with the language, I assumed he had not been long in the United States. What struck me with the taxi driver, and also with the child, was how easily bigotry is transmitted, not just across generations but cultures. Even in times of racial peace, that is a reality black parents dare not forget.

Youtha Hardman-Cromwell, a Methodist minister, mother of four, and university professor and administrator in Washington, D.C., says she would never encourage a black child to believe that America is color-blind. "I wouldn't . . . because there's too much racism that they have to face. And if they have no idea that that's what it is, then it looks crazy. Because they . . . can't understand why this [discrimination] is happening to them."

How does one teach a child about prejudice? "First of all," says Hardman-Cromwell, "you can tell your story. . . . They don't have to know all the details, but they need to know the story. . . . And they need to have a sense that you value them." In her eyes, to teach about prejudice is not the same as teaching children they are not responsible for their fate. Indeed, she believes almost the opposite, that children must be taught to distinguish between the things they can change and those they cannot: "We cannot project it all on other people, and yet we cannot take all the responsibility always ourselves. Sometimes it's us. Sometimes it's other people; and sometimes it's the system."

For parents, the lessons in race can extend well past their children's early years. Oliver Cromwell, Hardman-Cromwell's husband and a local government official, recalls having a long conversation with his son after a college teacher gave him a failing grade for being late with a paper. The son had talked with the instructor about an extension and thought that he had been granted a lengthy one. The teacher, however, remembered the conversation differently and refused to alter the grade. That incident, said Cromwell, led to his first talk with his son about the hazards of being black in a white environment, about not having "the luxury of depending on people's words, and taking people's word, and thinking that it's all going to be all right." Cromwell acknowledges that he had no way of knowing whether race was really an issue with the teacher, but he felt an obligation to share his own experience with discrimination—especially after concluding that his son's school, the University of Virginia, was anything but an oasis of racial tranquility: "Kids who went to UVA who thought they were in the mainstream of things found out very soon that they weren't, that there were a lot of things to overcome."

But even if one assumes that black children need to be taught to cope with the burden of race, how relevant is the experience of parents who were raised in a time when certain racial barriers were much higher than they are today, and in an era when racial attitudes now widely deemed unacceptable were freely exhibited without censure or embarrassment?

What is one to make, for instance, of the black law partner who laments that in today's gentler climate "white folks ain't saying what they mean," and who yearns for a return to the brutal honesty of the past, when it was very clear that "white people didn't like black folks"? Setting aside the question of whether those times were really as uncomplicated as he recalls, the very fact that he finds the present so discombobulating raises another more relevant possibility: that perhaps his own experience with racial limitations and discrimination can offer, at best, limited guidance for his children.

Growing up twenty, thirty, or forty years ago was simply not the same as growing up today, however similar certain 1990s indignities and social strictures may seem to older blacks, and however strong the parental urge may be to pass on painful yet essential truths.

As a youth in Danville, Illinois, in the late 1940s, for instance,

Joe Boyce saw bigotry the likes of which is rarely seen anywhere in America now. His mother, who had a master's degree and had taught at a prestigious black college in the South, could find no comparable work in Danville, so she settled for a job teaching in a black elementary school; and she made her accommodations to a system that devalued her as a human being.

When Boyce was a teenager, in the 1950s, his mother had a stroke. He and his brother had to work more than full time just to keep the household solvent. But what he remembers more clearly than the hard work—digging graves, washing dishes, and delivering newspapers—is the treatment his mother received in a hospital that refused to put black and white patients together. Because there was no "black" room available, his gravely ill mother was kept in a corridor—for which she paid the price of a room. The memory was so painful that Boyce had repressed it until he was talking with his own children about his mother one day and the images came flooding back. "I can't think about it now without wanting to cry," he says. "Every time I think about it I get mad all over again."

In some respects, Boyce's story is timeless; the sense of outrage at injustice and inequality, the pangs of helplessness while watching a loved one suffer, are things that transcend generations; yet the particular situation that evoked that pain is frozen in history. By the same token, the experience of Ulric Haynes, who came out of Yale University Law School in the 1950s, is not likely to be the experience of anyone graduating from Yale today. Haynes sent off 135 job applications and succeeded in getting interviews with more than seventy white firms, none of which was prepared to give him a job—even though there were jobs aplenty, as the country was in a period of relative prosperity. At one of the firms, he did manage to meet the sole black lawyer who seemed to have cracked the white wall. As Haynes recalls, the now-prominent attorney "sat me down and said, 'There's only room for one of us here, and I'm it.' "

"I've never forgotten it. And, in my heart of hearts, I've never really forgiven it," says Haynes, who acknowledges that the man was doing him something of a favor by telling him not to waste his time. But what rankles him still is the thought that the man was taking such delight in "doing the white man's bidding," in being "king shit."

While any number of "king shits" are still around, no one is in the same position as that lawyer of long ago, of being the sole black allowed to sit by the door in a branch of a profession that is keeping every other black out. Today no person of Haynes's training and talents is likely to find so many avenues of advance foreclosed or so many boundaries so clearly and rigidly defined. Today, when it comes to race, we are in uncharted waters. And between those who argue that nothing has changed and those who insist that everything has changed lies what most will recognize as the more complicated truth: that much indeed has changed since the fifties, and even since the sixties, but that we are incompetent to judge just how lasting, how important, and how far-reaching many of those changes are; that while some basic stereotypes remain very much in play, some formerly unbreakable barriers have crumbled. And for Haynes, Boyce, and millions of other black parents in America, that presents something of a problem, or at least a challenge: How can parents prepare children for reality's "rude awakening" while also preparing them for an array of possibilities infinitely grander than those enjoyed by their forebears? How can a parent who came up needing a ton of psychological armor instruct a child who may need only half a ton?

Terri Dickerson-Jones recalls that while growing up she had white friends with whom she could share anything, but that at some point things changed and she felt an incredible pressure to cast her lot with the white kids or stick with her fellow blacks. "I know it happened to me, and to all of my sisters. And it seems like it still happens. I worry about my son, whose best friend is white. Once people get to high school or college . . . it seems they're forced to choose one side or the other." She fears that the next generation and the one following are "destined to keep repeating the cycle," but she cannot be sure. She can at best try to prepare her son for what she believes he is likely to encounter.

The danger, of course, is that in preparing children for prejudice, in teaching them to protect themselves, parents may end up fortifying them against evils that no longer threaten, leaving them ill-prepared to take advantage of opportunities that they have been led not to expect, but that would loom large were it not for the blinders forged from lowered expectations. In the past, one "knew white people didn't like black folks," which is to say one knew how to act, how far one could go, and what would not be allowed. One knew that the color line, at some points, could never be crossed, and that it was worse than useless to try. In short, one knew one's place. For the parents of today, such certainty does not exist. Yet they still must help their children find their place in a world in which no one, white or black, knows precisely where that place will—or can—be.

chapter eight *White Racism, Black Racism, and the Search for Our Better Selves*

♦♦♦♦♦♦♦♦♦♦♦♦♦♦♦♦♦♦♦♦♦♦♦♦♦♦♦

$\mathcal{S}$HORTLY AFTER THE 1992 RIOTS IN LOS AN-geles, I was asked to appear on a panel before the U.S. Civil Rights Commission to address the subject of racial and ethnic tensions in America. Also on the panel were three prominent academics (two of them white), the director of a nonprofit institution, and another black journalist. It was not an especially memorable morning, as none of us said anything particularly profound; but I was struck that of the people testifying, it was the two white academics who were most insistent that white racism lies at the root of what ails black America.

That the whites were more outspoken than the blacks may simply reflect the passions of the specific individuals on the panel, but it may also reflect something more: that sophisticated blacks have learned that to suggest that whites are racist is not a useful exercise in the current climate—at least when talking to whites. Indeed, a murderer who blamed the devil for his crime would likely receive a more sympathetic hearing from many whites these days than would a black intellectual who railed against racism.

In the eyes of most whites, affluent blacks seem to have no real cause for complaint, and the problems faced by blacks in the underclass seem to have little to do with the actions or attitudes of whites. Street violence, abandoned families, and teenage pregnancies, it has been argued, are less the result of racism than of inner-city pathologies. To the extent that racism is perceived as a problem by whites, it is increasingly seen as an evil perpetrated by blacks—with whites (particularly Jews) serving principally as victims.

Ed Koch, the former mayor of New York, is a strong proponent of that view. When the subject of black-Jewish relations came up over lunch in late 1992, at a time when these relations seemed even more frayed than usual in New York, Koch cited a "shocking statistic" from a recent local poll indicating that 63 percent of blacks were anti-Semitic. Koch brushed aside my questioning of the statistic by arguing that the pollster had designed the question-naire, not he: "I don't know whether it's good or bad; I'm not a pollster. But they've used it every year."

At any rate, Koch quickly abandoned the poll to focus on Brooklyn's Crown Heights, a neighborhood that at several points in the recent past had been the focus of black-Jewish, racial-religious conflict. In Koch's eyes, the ongoing strife was partly a consequence of the shortage of housing and other resources in the area: "The Hasidim have families of ten to fifteen kids. They have been told by the Rebbe that they must live in this area. They must walk to the synagogue, therefore they can't spread out. . . . The blacks who moved into the area . . . which, was once a very prosperous white Jewish community . . . they too are under strain in terms of meeting their housing. So there is that competition."

But tight resources accounted only for part of the problem, said Koch. Race-based resentments also played a role: "The Jews feel beleaguered and angry . . . because they're the only white group that stayed. You can't find white groups remaining in areas where blacks move in and become the dominant group. Whites move out. The Jews stayed and they think maybe the city ought to give them a little credit for that, including the black community. In-stead, they get a lot of resentment. 'Why don't you move' is one of the things that is said to them."

Such resentment, Koch went on to argue, is not directed only at the Hasidim but at Jews in general. "When I was mayor, you had . . . [Congressman] Charlie Rangel threaten the Jewish com-munity. . . . I will take you back ten years, when he referred to me as Bull Connor publicly, when he called me king of the Jews, which is a divisive, blasphemous term. . . . No one said a word. I said, 'Is no one going to defend me?' "

That black-Jewish relations should have deteriorated so badly is not something Koch finds terribly shocking, for he does not believe there ever really was much of a "special relationship" between blacks and Jews. Certainly, among the black and Jewish leadership of the civil rights movement, there were some extremely close ties. And certainly, many Jewish individuals, including Koch, got involved in civil rights because it seemed the moral thing to do. But he would have done the same, said Koch, if Eskimos had been the group whose rights were threatened. Moreover, whatever the connection between blacks and Jews in the past, it is the present that primarily concerns him; and that present, as he sees it, is largely defined by a double standard that permits blacks to make racist or anti-Semitic attacks on Jews, attacks that very few groups, including the recognized Jewish leadership ("Court Jews who like to have coffee with the czar or the mayor at Gracie Mansion," scoffs Koch), dare to oppose. Koch's are strong sentiments, but they are not atypical. He is only one of many who are fed up with what they see as a new tolerance of black racists and anti-Semites.

But while Koch's complaint is not without foundation, neither is it fully accurate. The "shocking statistic" he cites comes from a 1992 Roper Organization survey for the American Jewish Committee that did not pretend to measure anti-Semitism. It did find that 63 percent of black respondents thought Jews had "too much influence in New York City life and politics." The same survey also found that 23 percent of Jews (and 18 percent of whites) thought blacks had "too much influence"—which, by Koch's reasoning, would make nearly a fourth of New York's Jews racist.

Another poll, commissioned by the Anti-Defamation League, did attempt to track anti-Semitism, though without claiming to measure anti-Semitism directly. Instead, it listed a series of statements describing Jewish stereotypes or common preconceptions about Jews that interviewees designated as true or false.

(1) Jews stick together more than other Americans. (2) Jews always like to be at the head of things. (3) Jews are more loyal to Israel than America. (4) Jews have too much power in the U.S. today. (5) Jews have too much control and influence on Wall

Street.   (6) Jews have too much power in the business world.
(7) Jews have a lot of irritating faults.   (8) Jews are more willing than others to use shady practices to get what they want.
(9) Jewish businessmen are so shrewd that others don't have a fair
chance in competition.   (10) Jews don't care what happens to
anyone but their own kind.   (11) Jews are [not] just as honest as
other businessmen. [Bracketed "not" in original.]

Respondents who gave stereotypical responses to six or more of
the statements were judged "most anti-Semitic." The survey, released in November 1992 and conducted by Marttila & Kiley Inc.,
found that 37 percent of black Americans and 17 percent of white
Americans fit into the "most anti-Semitic" category. It also found
that well-educated blacks, like well-educated whites, were less
likely to buy into such stereotypes.

While the Roper and Marttila & Kiley surveys show a high
incidence of prejudice and unfortunate stereotypes, they do not
exactly show that most blacks are anti-Jewish. And they certainly
don't show that most blacks are antiwhite. What they do show is
something a good deal more complex. The Roper survey, for
instance, found that blacks rated Jews higher in intelligence than
blacks and thought Jews less likely to be lazy or to "prefer to live
off welfare." Jews themselves came essentially to the same conclusions, but by larger margins. Whites (including Jews) rated
Jews as more intelligent, less lazy, and less likely to prefer welfare
than blacks, and ranked the Irish and Italians between Jews and
blacks on all three traits.

Both surveys indicate (especially after allowing for group chauvinism and ideologically correct though dishonest responses) that
Americans are in substantial agreement about their stereotypes.
In other words, even black racists and black anti-Semites generally see Jews as bright, ambitious, powerful, and capable people.
Conversely, most whites, even those who harbor African Americans no ill-will, tend to see blacks as significantly less intelligent
and less motivated than whites.

To those inclined to see black and white racism as different
sides of the same coin, the implications should be obvious. While

any stereotype is bad, all stereotypes are not the same, either in their conception or in their consequences. A stereotype that casts a group as superior is very different from one that renders a group inferior. To recognize that is to realize that while white racism and black racism and anti-Semitism are all evil things, they do not lead to the same place or spring from the same stream.

As the Anti-Defamation League says in its report, much of the response to the question of whether Jews have "too much power" is complicated by a widespread perception among blacks that whites in general have too much power. Indeed, when a similar question was asked in a 1992 survey by the *Los Angeles Times* ("Do you think any one of these groups—Whites, Asians, blacks, or Latinos—is getting more economic power than is good for Los Angeles?"), 36 percent of blacks thought whites were too powerful, and 43 percent thought the same of Asians. To conclude from that that 36 percent of black Angelenos are antiwhite and 43 percent anti-Asian would be to make a huge and unjustifiable leap. No doubt some true racists, xenophobes, and anti-Semites were among those polled, but far outnumbering them were a great many people whose response to the survey can be best understood as a plaintive plea, as a way of asking, "Isn't it time that *we* got some power, instead of seeing it go to all these others?"

Such sentiments, composed largely of envy, anger, and resentment, are not necessarily inappropriate to the condition in which many blacks find themselves. The problem is that those feelings can sometimes harden into hatred of Asians, whites, or Jews—especially if inflamed by demagogues or pseudoscholars who make certain groups responsible for all the sins of the world. Even that hatred, however, is principally a defensive hatred: the hatred of those who have been kept out. Black racists, for instance, do not generally believe that whites are unintelligent, lazy, or incompetent—at least not *because* they are white.

The animosity blacks experience from white racists is different. It is the animosity of people who presume themselves to be superior—morally, intellectually, physically, or perhaps in all three ways—and who cannot countenance a world in which that presumption is not shared.

It is right to recognize both brands of racial hostility as problems. It is wrong, however, to assume that the solution is simply to urge people to get along, or somehow to mix members of one camp in with the other. For even if racial peace is maintained, the web of stereotypes is left untouched, and those stereotypes, as already noted, are particularly destructive to blacks. They not only encourage whites to treat blacks as inferiors but also encourage blacks to see themselves as many whites would have them be.

These stereotypes spew forth from every segment of popular culture and constantly find new life in black and nonblack communities across America. Rap music, for instance, routinely portrays black men as "niggaz" and "gangstas" and black women as "bitches" and "hos." A host of black comedians follow suit, depicting a jive-talking, foul-mouthed, illiterate stud who defines the essence of "black" for many young people. Attachment to this stereotype is so powerful that African Americans who choose not to personify it are often accused by other blacks of trying not to be black. Yet those with a sense of history know that the stud image did not spring from the black community but originated with whites searching for signs that blacks were intellectually inferior and morally degenerate—and therefore suitable for use as slaves. Today, through television, movies, and the innumerable interracial encounters that occur in an increasingly integrated society, blacks and whites in effect conspire to determine whether, and to what extent, the stereotypes can change—in short, what the place of African Americans will be.

Unlike recent immigrants, who are relatively free to define their own place in U.S. society, African Americans are more constrained. John Ogbu, an anthropologist at the University of California, Berkeley, who has studied immigrant and indigenous minorities, writes: "Immigrants generally regard themselves as foreigners, 'strangers' who come to America with expectation of certain economic, political, and social benefits. While anticipating that such benefits might come at some cost . . . the immigrants did not measure their success or failure primarily by the standards of white Americans, but by the standards of their homelands. Such minorities, at least during the first generation, did not internalize

the effects of such discrimination, of cultural and intellectual deni-
gration. . . . Even when they were restricted to manual labor, they
did not consider themselves to be occupying the lowest rung of the
American status system, and partly because they did not fully
understand that system, and partly because they did not consider
themselves as belonging to it, they saw their situation as temporary.''

In contrast, Ogbu says, he has observed black and Mexican-
American parents encouraging their children to do well in school
while unconsciously passing on another, more demoralizing message: ''Unavoidably, such minority parents discuss their problems
with 'the system,' with their relatives, friends, and neighbors in
the presence of their children. The result . . . is that such children
become increasingly disillusioned about their ability to succeed in
adult life through the mainstream strategy of schooling.'' The only
way some of these kids feel they can succeed, he concludes, is to
''repudiate their black peers, black identity, and black cultural
frames of reference.''

Few people of any race, of course, have the strength, desire,
imagination, or appetite to abandon ideas they have been taught
all their lives. Thus, Americans of all races continue to see each
other through a prism of distorting colors, and to struggle with the
problem of prejudice.

Joe Feagin, a University of Florida sociologist who has exten-
sively studied the black middle class (and who was one of those on
the U.S. Civil Rights Commission panel mentioned above), believes that even the subtle displays of prejudice blacks today are
more likely to encounter can be devastating. ''Today white discrimination less often involves blatant door-slamming exclusion,
for many blacks have been allowed in the corporate door. Modern
discrimination more often takes the form of tracking, limiting or
blocking promotions, harassment, and other differential treatment signalling disrespect.'' The result, writes Feagin, is the ''restriction, isolation, and ostracism of middle-class blacks who have
penetrated the traditionally white workplace'' but who find that
they are not part of the same networks that ''link together not only
white co-workers but also white supervisors and, in some situa-

tions, clients." And this more subtle form of exclusion produces repressed rage, inner conflict, and a deep sense of dissatisfaction: "Most middle-class blacks are caught between the desire for the American dream imbedded deeply in their consciousness and a recognition that the dream is white at its heart."

Derrick Bell, civil rights activist and legal scholar, has a perspective that is even more dispiriting than Feagin's. In *Faces at the Bottom of the Well*, Bell argues that America's brand of racism is permanent and that we must set aside the hopelessly idealistic notion that time and generosity will cure it. Since whites will never recognize blacks as equals, blacks must steel themselves for never-ending struggle: "African Americans must confront and conquer the otherwise deadening reality of our permanent subordinate status. Only in this way can we prevent ourselves from being dragged down by society's racial hostility."

In an epilogue titled "Beyond Despair," Bell invokes inspirational images from the time of slavery, when black people, "knowing there was no escape, no way out, . . . nonetheless continued to engage themselves. To carve out a humanity. To defy the murder of selfhood. Their lives were brutally shackled, certainly—but *not without meaning despite being imprisoned*." He argues that blacks today, in accepting their tragic fate, should take a cue from the slaves who managed to beat the odds "with absolutely nothing to help—save imagination, will, and unbelievable strength and courage."

In outlining his controversial thesis Bell throws out a challenge, declaring that the proposition of permanent inequality "will be easier to reject than refute." That is certainly true, for it is a prediction about the future, which by definition has not yet arrived and hence is impossible to describe with certainty. But that does not make Bell's gloomy prognosis correct.

To be sure, there are abundant signs that the concept of equality is under siege: in the popularity of such people as race-baiter David Duke, who lost his bid to be governor of Louisiana but managed to get the majority of the white vote; in the frequency of so-called bias or hate crimes; in the avalanche of academic and government studies that document chronic discrimination in housing, banking, employment, and virtually every other aspect of American life; and in the painful and yet persistent debate over whether, as former Los Angeles Dodgers general manager Al Campanis put it, blacks possess "the necessities" for leadership.

The Campanis spirit periodically reemerges with a vengeance— as it did recently in the person of Marge Schott, owner of the Cincinnati Reds. In 1993 Schott's widely reported comments (she referred, for instance, to "dumb, lazy niggers" and "money-grub-bing Jews") won her a one-year suspension from baseball and a $25,000 fine. Schott had never hired a minority person for any of the forty-five positions in her front office; but her more serious crime, it seems, was not keeping her insulting opinions to herself, or at least within the owners' circle, where baseball writers claim such opinions are widely shared.

In a blistering attack on the owners for their seemingly hypo-critical treatment of Schott, *New York Times* columnist Ira Ber-kow wrote: "They have no business coming down on her for racial and ethnic slurs that were uttered in private, something, to be sure, some if not many of them have said in one way or another themselves. And if they haven't said it, they have certainly acted as though they believe such racial and ethnic stereotypes are written in stone, or at least the baseball bylaws."

Whether or not Berkow's assertion is true, the fact that blacks' basic abilities are constantly questioned, in all circles of society, is not a matter of much dispute. And nowhere has that questioning been so persistent as in the arena of academic achievement, where those whose basic competencies are in doubt are provided the opportunity to prove the skeptics wrong. The problem, of course, is that for all the individual examples of black academic brilliance, many blacks have performed quite poorly in school and on the standardized tests that are the touchstone of the academy. There has been a relatively small but significant difference between how blacks and whites, on average, score on those tests; and that difference has helped fuel an ongoing debate, not only over whether blacks are in some sense intellectually inferior, but over whether that conjectured inferiority has a genetic base.

I am among those who believe that the test scores shed light on a real difference in academic achievement—and one that cannot be dismissed purely as a function of cultural bias. Anyone who has spent much time in predominantly black public schools knows that education is not always a priority in such institutions. In some places things are much as they were when I was a schoolboy and heard one teacher say that blacks had "lazy tongues," and another announce that he didn't care whether anyone learned anything since he was getting paid anyway, and yet another explain, when challenged over handing out brain-deadening assignments, that kids like us were incapable of handling difficult material. Scholastic attainment may not generally be discouraged in so brutal a manner, but legions of black kids still have it instilled in them that they are not particularly intelligent; and at least partly as a result of such indoctrination, many give up on academic achievement at a very young age. I see that as a serious problem for our society, and for our schools. But I am not inclined to believe that it means African Americans have some genetic deficiency that renders most of them less capable than most whites.

Over the years, various researchers have tried to determine whether (or to what extent) environment or genetics accounts for the difference, with less than conclusive results. For one thing, with all the genetic mixing that has gone on, it's not at all clear what "black" and "white" races mean in any scientific sense. Moreover, to try to tease out the genetic component by comparing blacks and whites from the same environment is not an easy task. Even if a black group and a white group seem equally poor, equally ill-educated, and equally nurtured (or neglected) by their parents, how can one establish that the environments were truly the same? Could there not still be what author Daniel Seligman calls an "X factor," something that "goes with the experience of being black in America" that would make the black-white comparisons moot?

Seligman raises the possibility only to dismiss it, noting that numerous experts find the proposition "excessively mysterious," and blithely going on to make the case for a difference rooted in the genes. In truth, neither proposition can be proved. But even if the so-called X factor cannot be easily grasped or quantified, that surely doesn't demonstrate that it doesn't exist. And citing a number of experts swimming in a sea of admitted ignorance about intelligence in general does not make the genetics argument any more compelling, especially given that those experts are part of a society that is in profound denial concerning matters of discrimination and race.

The possibility of a special burden born of "the experience of being black in America" is anything but mysterious to blacks. Blacks fully understand that to be an African American is in many respects to be uniquely branded for failure. It is to grow up constantly being told, in the schools and in the streets, that blacks are not as bright as whites and are not academically inclined. Adjusting for economic class differences alone is not sufficient to address the difference in experiences. In order even to begin to make a decent comparison across groups, one would have to find either a group of whites who had been constantly discouraged, since they were toddlers, from trying to develop anything remotely resembling an intellect, or a group of blacks who had always been told that they are the best and brightest in the world, and never doubted it.

This is not to say that studies of race and intelligence (or whatever it is that IQ tests really measure) should not be carried out. They probably should, and could no doubt, yield some fascinating data. But even more useful might be an experiment that would try to determine why the nation is in such a state of denial, why so many whites find it so hard to believe that blacks experience what blacks clearly do. Such an experiment might well yield some practical remedies instead of new and necessarily speculative theories on the genetics of the IQ gap. For even if we could prove that many blacks are genetically programmed to do poorly on standardized tests, where would that lead us? Certainly not to the conclusion that blacks should not be educated. The United States, after all, has already tried that policy, and with disastrous results. Furthermore, however blacks do on average, many individual blacks would continue to test much higher than individual whites. And even were that not so, would society be willing to make the case that performance on a standardized test is the most relevant measure of worth?

Still, the fact that many choose to believe that genetics explains the gap is revealing—not so much of the state of science, but of the believers' state of mind. It is not such a great step from accept-ing the proposition that blacks suffer from genetic mediocrity to accepting the even more controversial corollary: that whatever condition blacks find themselves in is not the fault—or respon-sibility—of society at large, and certainly not of whites, but is primarily attributable to an inherent flaw.

If such a thing could in fact be established, the political hay to be reaped in certain quarters is obvious. For the finding would be received as a strong argument for the status quo. It would make clear, for instance, that the reason so few blacks are in upper management is that so few are capable of managing. And it would explain why many whites are entirely justified in not wishing their children to marry blacks. It would bolster those who argue that affirmative action necessarily results in a decline in quality. And it would excuse centuries of abuse and neglect of a people whose gravest offense was wishing to be treated as Americans. It would even lend respectability to the arguments of those who say, in effect, that America is not one country but at least two, and that because those two countries are separate and innately different, the fate of one should be severed from that of the other.

I am not suggesting that anyone interested in genetics and intelligence has an explicitly political agenda. Science has left any number of questions unanswered—including many of the nature/ nurture sort—and all are fair game for legitimate investigation. Yet it would be naive to assume that it is merely scientific curiosity that has driven certain intellectuals, ever since the dawn of black slavery, to search for defensible criteria by which to declare blacks inherently deficient. That the assumption of deficiency has been so persistent, even in the absence of proof, is an indication that this particular issue may be driven more by rationalizations than sci-ence—the same class of rationalizations that have been used throughout America's history to deny blacks a full role in Ameri-can life.

Many who have been on the receiving end of such specious assumptions have found themselves in the same boat as Derrick Bell: concluding that blacks have always been—and always will be—relegated to a permanent inferior caste. Yet for all Bell's arguments to the contrary, his solution strikes many as little more than a prescription for despair. The Zenlike state of mental resistance he endorses is not something many individuals are likely to attain. And even if they could, I suspect that most blacks these days are not interested in walking in the spectral footsteps of long-dead slaves—which is not to say they are uninterested in the lessons of the past, but that they are even more interested in the possibilities of the future.

As Mary Curtis, the *New York Times* editor, observed, "You always want to think things are going to be better." Moreover, there is plenty of time to reach the conclusion that America is beyond redemption, and there is little harm in proceeding as if it were not. As Bill Bradley says, "I respect Derrick Bell a lot, but I'm not at that point yet where I think this is a permanent destructive aspect of American culture that can never be overcome. . . . This is not something that you're going to give up on because it's difficult."

Bradley, of course, is white, and as he quickly acknowledges, he has not walked in Bell's shoes or fought at the same barricades as Bell: "He's battled . . . a lot longer and in a much different way than I." Yet the argument for rejecting Bell's dismal prognosis is not dependent on color, or even on experience, but on a simple and hard-nosed approach to reality: if people are destined to spend their lives in struggle, they might as well struggle against a real evil instead of fighting merely to maintain their humanity in the face of continued disrespect. Moreover, maintaining one's humanity—indeed, even drawing strength from being battered by prejudice and rejection—need not be dependent on giving up hope that America can be better. As associate Judge Ricardo Urbina of the Superior Court of the District of Columbia observes, "The very things that made me vulnerable made me strong."

Urbina, the black American son of a Honduran father and Puerto Rican mother, grew up in Queens, New York, where he took abuse from all sides. Living in Jackson Heights among Italian and Irish immigrants, he was initially taken to be black—which he was, but he was also Hispanic. So at times he felt "betwixt and between. . . . At times I was made to feel uncomfortable by all three groups"—blacks, whites, and Hispanics.

A star athlete, Urbina got to Georgetown University on a track scholarship in the 1960s, when there were "only a couple of us." And he saw his athletic excellence as a weapon: "I expected it to neutralize some of the . . . negative stereotypes that I knew white society was capable of inflicting on me." But he also knew that he had to be a good student: "I knew from very early on that I needed to do more than others, white people, who would be similarly situated. . . . I knew I had to do very well athletically, well academically. I had to get along."

"Did I feel racial discrimination? Yes I did," says Urbina, but notes that it was not enough to deter him, though one incident in particular stayed with him. It occurred not on school grounds but at a club in the Marriott Hotel, where he had gone with some white friends after a dance. A young redneck type confronted him in the bar, and Urbina tried to defuse the situation by leaving; but the man and his friends followed Urbina to his car, and in the end Urbina knocked the guy to the ground. When the police came, instead of arresting the aggressor and his two friends, they grabbed Urbina and tossed him in the police car. Only the intervention of a cashier who happened to witness the entire incident prevented his arrest. It was a powerful lesson about race—one of many Urbina accumulated along the way. Yet he says, "I don't think I'm bitter or angry . . . but I'm always very vigilant." His vigilance against discrimination is all the more heightened because he has children and hopes they will be spared the uglier side of intolerance.

Urbina is a remarkable man, yet in many respects he's typical of those I talked to for this book: people who have managed, while hurdling barriers most whites rarely notice, to find the time and drive to lead distinguished lives. Ulric Haynes, the Hofstra dean, recalled a conversation he had with a white colleague. "I said, . . . 'You don't understand at the end of the day I'm twice as tired as you are, because I face all the problems that you face plus the special challenges that I face as a black in a key position in this institution. One set of problems is . . . draining. Two sets of problems is twice as . . . draining."

It is worth considering the strategies Haynes and his similarly accomplished peers have used to make work less draining and to overcome the obstacles fate has strewn in their way—not only because those strategies may help others, but because they provide some insight into how high a price many successful blacks have paid to get where they are.

Before Haynes could become a success, he first had to deal with his considerable anger over his rejection by the law establishment. When Haynes got his law degree from Yale in 1956, he thought the world was his for the taking: "I got suckered into believing that because I performed as well as anybody else . . . opportunities were going to be as available to me as they were to them." He still keeps a packet of the turndown letters he received from major law firms, just to remind him of what those days were like. "The excuses were standard. The nice ones were, 'Oh, you wouldn't be happy with us.' The nasty ones were, 'Well our clients would feel uncomfortable dealing with someone of your race.' In between were those that said, 'You're certainly overqualified for anything we have to offer . . .' To finish the sentence, *'anything we have to offer someone of your race.'* I made one hundred and thirty five job applications. I had seventy-seven interviews and got one job offer."

Haynes naturally found the experience intensely painful, and he was forced to turn his back on the legal career he had planned to pursue. But in the midst of rejection, he also found the instrument of his deliverance: "Fortunately, the one job offer I got came from Averill Harriman, who was then governor of New York State, and it was through him that I embarked on a career in international affairs. . . . It was very important to me, given my frustration in my own country, that I get out of my country. And I joined the staff of the United Nations secretariat in the European office in Geneva, Switzerland. . . . Then, from there, I went to the Ford Foundation in Nigeria, and then in Tunisia, at a time when both of those countries were newly independent. It was not by accident that I stayed abroad as long as I did. Or that I still frequently seek opportunities to go abroad. Living and working abroad helped me to come to terms with the disappointment I had known in my own country. And to turn what might have been self-destructive rage into rather more productive energy." Instead of self-destructing, he found himself vowing, "I'll show the sons of bitches. I'll distinguish myself where they can't touch me."

Temporary escape from America is not an option for everyone, but other strategies Haynes learned through the years have broader utility. "Early on, when I was a visiting lecturer at the Harvard Business School," says Haynes, "I used to tell [African Americans], 'For the love of God, do not accept a staff position if it is offered to you in a major corporation. They are dead-end positions.' I also told them to avoid the human resource function, or the 'personnel function,' as it was known then. Avoid community relations. Avoid special markets. Those are all euphemisms for 'black executive positions.' Don't get into corporate giving. Don't get sidetracked into the corporate foundation. You don't move from these positions up the promotional ladder."

Haynes would also tell his young protégés to watch their behavior—and their attitude: "When a young white . . . male executive enters a corporation at the entry level and he's aggressive, he's called ambitious. When a young black does the same, he's called many things, none of which are flattering. He is 'not a team player' or 'has expectations that outpace the reality of the company to deliver.' The same behavior in two individuals is valued in a different way, or judged in a different way. Recognize the fact, don't necessarily accept it, deal with it as the reality. But don't say . . . that 'that has to prevent me from getting ahead.' " Look at it instead as "one of the obstacles that I have to contend with. Race . . . is one of the obstacles. . . . I must never forget that. But it is, like every other obstacle, one that I can overcome."

Darwin Davis, senior vice president of the Equitable Life Assurance Society, thinks that "one of the . . . fastest, most direct, most sure ways [to success] is to get involved in a company where you're selling." Certainly coming up through sales worked for him—largely, he suspects, because sales provided a relatively objective measure of worth, and a counterbalance to the subjective evaluations that can kill minority employees' careers. Instead of a supervisor's opinions, he had "marks on a board." And that, he believes, made all the difference. A black law partner made much the same point: "You can protect yourself by becoming valuable . . . figuring out what is the bottom line."

Harvard psychiatrist Alvin Poussaint emphasizes the need to build alliances, both within and outside the organization, and especially with other blacks. Among other things, a group of employees can criticize the organization and suggest improvements in a way that a single employee perhaps cannot, thus minimizing the risk a black person expressing "individual anger" is always subject to, in Poussaint's view. Another advantage of seeking out others, says Poussaint, is that they may offer a sympathetic ear because they are experiencing the same frustrations. Some blacks, he notes, "don't understand where [their conflicted feelings] are coming from themselves." Some, perhaps, think that what they are undergoing is unique. The opportunity to discuss their experiences and emotions with others can at times be invaluable.

Psychologist and management consultant Ron Brown also believes it is important for black professionals to find a "reality check," someone they trust, of any race, who can assure them that they are not going crazy when the racial demons strike. Sometimes, says Brown, that function can be served by informal groups, or by counterparts in other organizations whom a black executive feeling under siege might ask, "Am I off base here? . . . What's your experience?"

Many of the other people I interviewed had had insights or experienced personal epiphanies that made it a bit easier for them or someone they cared about to achieve success. And sometimes those insights concerned matters that seem almost trivial. Basil Paterson, for instance, recalls a conversation he had with former Manhattan borough president Percy Sutton when Paterson was making his first race for statewide office in New York. Sutton asked him why he didn't smile in any of his pictures. Paterson

replied that he had always looked angry when running in a predominantly black district and that he had always done just fine.
Sutton told him he had better smile when running statewide.

Donald McHenry says he learned long ago to see a virtue where
others might see a disadvantage. From his earliest days in the
Foreign Service, he told himself, "Sure, I stand out because of
race," but that was not necessarily bad. "There are a thousand
young white boys who have exactly the same background, the
same abilities as I do," he observes, "but in this circumstance,
with this one thousand, I have one advantage"—his conspicuous-
ness. Others had other advantages, and in McHenry's book, that
was simply a fact of life. "John Q., who . . . is white, has one
thousand people who have the exact background, the same
capabilities as he does, but his father went to school with Joe
Blow. That's *his* one advantage. Or his parents were able to take
him on a European trip, and he learned French, or Spanish, or
what have you." Some students had to spend a great deal of time
looking for the one thing that would make their résumés different:
"I was born with mine, provided I made sure I was as good as that
other thousand. I tried like hell to be as good. . . . I was in
pioneering areas. There weren't many people in foreign affairs.
Do you find yourself carrying a burden? Only if you think of it in
racial terms. I don't carry on my shoulders the burden of race. *I
don't do it*. I know that if I fall on my face there will be those who
will look on it in racial terms, but I don't . . . at least at this stage."

Francine Soliunas, counsel for Illinois Bell, advises blacks to
make a special effort to get whites in the corporation to view them
as complete human beings: "You have to begin to allow other
people to understand you in order that they are not threatened by
you, and that they realize that you have kids like they do, that you
go to church . . . that you do all the things that they do, maybe not
with the same people. Until we begin to understand that allowing
ourselves to do that is not a threat to us or to our blackness, we
are not going to infiltrate."

But even those who successfully "infiltrate" the corporate culture sometimes find it an extremely uncongenial place and continue to be haunted by demons, anxieties, and anger that white

executives simply don't have to endure. And black executives, notes Ron Brown, often must suffer in silence. "There are very few places where, if you want to be successful, you can express that outrage." While many white executives might simply insist on an end to the things that were bothering them, Brown wonders how many black executives would declare, for instance, that racial jokes in the department must stop. It's extremely hard, he says, for a black executive "to deal with an organizational outrage that just happens to be racial."

Ella Bell, of the Sloan School of Management at MIT, also believes that many blacks find it virtually impossible to cope with affronts within the corporation on their own, and has concluded that perhaps they should look outside for help: "There are very few places in society for us to really do . . . in-depth work on these issues. And I'm convinced it's not [within] corporations. . . . We need to do this kind of work in our communities, in our churches, in our schools. We [need] a safe place to do the work, for blacks to deal with the kinds of conceptions and the consequences, both the good and the bad, of our racial identities. . . . And whites definitely have very few whites to even lead that dialogue for them."

The fact is that neither blacks nor whites, in any substantial numbers, are prepared to go into the wilderness to deal with racial issues. They will be dealt with as a part of everyday life, and in the context of the everyday world. In that world the workplace remains the most common location where large numbers of minority and white adults come into contact with each other. That is not likely to change anytime soon, so for the foreseeable future what happens on the job will continue to have an enormous bearing on how Americans of all colors think about race.

At present it's difficult to find anyone who truly believes that race relations are good in most American corporations. Minorities, and blacks in particular, think they have gotten a raw deal, that even though the gates of the corporation have swung open, many doors are still marked "whites only." At the same time, armies of white men have convinced themselves—or been convinced—that marginally competent minorities, pushed along by quotas, are snatching up every decent job and promotion in sight, leaving nothing worth having to hardworking whites who only want a fair shake.

It is no exaggeration to say that much of corporate America is in a personnel crisis. Affirmative action, once regarded as a solution, has proven to be a magnet for resentment and criticism. Even those sympathetic to its goals are no longer singing its praises. Instead, many have shifted ground and are now touting what they call "management of diversity," an evolving doctrine that proponents hope to erect on the decaying carcass of affirmative action.

Management consultant Roosevelt Thomas, founder of the American Institute for Managing Diversity, made the case in an influential 1990 article in the *Harvard Business Review*. Thomas argued that five premises on which affirmative action rests are badly in need of revision, as follows: (1) though in the past white males made up the business world mainstream, today they themselves are a statistical minority; (2) the U.S. economy, which formerly seemed stable and flourishing, with room to absorb all comers, is now scrambling to adapt; (3) prejudice, which was responsible for keeping minorities out, has either wasted away or been effectively suppressed; (4) whereas once companies had to be forced—through legal and social coercion—to recruit minorities, they are now delighted to do so; (5) women and minorities, who were formerly in need of a "boarding pass" are now in need of "an upgrade."

Affirmative action played its role well, says Thomas, but its time is nearly at an end. Ultimately it cannot help many people win promotions because "it is perceived to conflict with the meritocracy we favor." Nor does it provide much guidance for those of the younger generation who would prefer to be something other than tokens: "A black vice president who got her job through affirmative action is not necessarily a model of how to rise through the corporate meritocracy. She may be a model of how affirmative action can work for the people who find or put themselves in the right place at the right time."

Instead of focusing on affirmative action, which in Thomas's formulation means focusing explicitly on race and the advancement of minorities and women, he suggests that employers affirm diversity, which means asking, "Given the diverse work force I've got, am I getting the productivity, does it work as smoothly, is morale as high, as if every person in the company was the same sex and race and nationality?" The difference between the two mindsets, Thomas says, is enormous; rather than narrowly concerning itself with equality for women and minorities, the new approach aims to make the workplace function fairly and effectively for everyone. Moreover, he argues, "diversity" does not imply a lowering of standards, but instead a greater recognition of competence.

How does the theory work in action? It's too early to say. At best, there are anecdotal reports, such as the one I received from an employee relations executive at one of America's largest companies. She was not authorized to speak for the company, so I will not use her name. Nonetheless, the story of her experience is worth passing along.

The company, which had long prided itself on its equal opportunity efforts, was intrigued by U.S. Labor Department projections indicating that America's workers would increasingly be women, ethnic minorities, and immigrants. When company executives looked at those projections in relation to their own future work force, they found, as expected, that it would probably mirror the national pattern. What they did not expect to find was evidence of managerial favoritism and a looming manpower crisis. Yet a close look at the data revealed that women and minorities were not being promoted at anything like the rates to be expected, either as a proportion of their total numbers or as a function of their performance appraisals. Moreover, they were leaving the company at an alarming rate.

The employee relations executive was so disturbed by the findings that she sought permission to probe further. In making the case for the inquiry, she scrupulously avoided the phrase "glass ceiling" or any other language that might imply that management was insensitive or unfairly blocking people's careers. Such catch-words, she figured, would more likely trigger excuses than ap-proval for her proposal.

Once authorized to proceed, she organized several focus groups on the basis of ethnicity and gender—i.e., Hispanic, Asian-American, and black males in one group, females in another; and white males in one group, females in another. She made a point of selecting some of the best performers in the company, people about whom it could not be said that they were incompetents or chronic malcontents. After assembling the groups, she asked each whether the firm was in fact the kind of organization management presumed it to be: a place where employees could do their best work and be rewarded for their contributions to the company. For the most part, the white males said that it was. The minorities and females were not so sure.

Nothing the employees said in the focus groups really surprised her; what they said afterwards did. Following the sessions they were allowed to respond confidentially (by writing down their answers and placing them in a ballot box) to the following ques-tions: "Has there ever been an occasion when you were judged on a basis other than merit? And what was it like?" She had expected some fairly mild anecdotes; what she got was a jolting barrage—detailed cases of sexual harassment and blatant racial discrimina-tion, and a flood of simmering resentment. She found much of the material shocking but was struck most of all by the fact that despite the awful things people reported, they still thought the company was a generally good place to work. To her it was as though they were saying, " 'We're accustomed to this treatment,' which I found very sad on some level. Their expectations were so low."

The disgruntlement, she discovered, affected every group in the company, not only females and blacks. White men suspected age discrimination or were convinced that women and minorities were getting all the top jobs. Given the company's statistical pro-file, that perception was absurd, but it was nonetheless genuine. As she mulled over the mournful messages that had poured into the ballot box, she realized something else about the corporate culture—that people who had worked for the company for years still "didn't feel comfortable bringing complaints."

When she reported her findings to management, the initial reaction was denial. "How can this be?" she heard again and again. "Those people must have axes to grind." But she pointed out that it was very unlikely that several hundred employees, most of them high performers, could all have ulterior motives. "These are not the malcontents," she would stress. "These are not the poorly rated. This is what the people who like it here say. And when you look at good people who talk about these incidents, you can't simply ignore them."

The corporation's chief executive thought of himself as a progressive boss who had gone out of his way to develop women and minorities. "Our study completely changed the view he had of himself," she says, and made it possible for her to launch a series of follow-up projects.

In later meetings, she helped to persuade minorities and women that their complaints were being seriously addressed. And she helped the white men to see that their perceptions were in error, that women and minorities were not getting most of the top jobs but in fact were getting very few of them. She encouraged them to explore the reasons for the dearth of minority managers and patiently pulled apart, one by one, the rationalizations given for the slow pace of minority progress. She showed that contrary to their assumptions, the women and minorities were technically proficient and had put in, by and large, just as many years as the white males who were being promoted above them. She also tried to persuade the men that through "managing diversity" well— which is to say, ensuring that all employees would be judged by common criteria, and that competence and effort, not management's preconceptions, would determine who got ahead—everyone in the company would eventually benefit.

The chief executive officer made the message his own and began promoting management of diversity at every opportunity. The early returns are encouraging, the employee relations executive says. There is more of a sense within the company that competence counts and that complaints will be heeded; more women and minorities seem to be moving up the chain of command.

Whether these trends will continue over time, whether "management of diversity" is in fact a way to make "equal opportunity" palatable, are not questions I feel competent to answer. The jury is a long way from being in. But clearly, just to get the process started, the people in the above-mentioned company had to work through layer upon layer of misconceptions, defenses, and rationalizations. The chief executive and his key lieutenants had to force themselves to look at the corporation anew—to see past the assumption, which happened not to be true, that they had established a meritocracy in which everyone, including women and minorities, could do their best work. Jettisoning such preconceptions is no easy task, and it is one that many people have neither the imagination, intellectual honesty, nor will to accomplish.

Ulric Haynes, for one, maintains, "We're still going through that denial stage. . . . In a way it's like the Germans with respect to the Holocaust. The German nation is going through that kind of denial. And most white people in the United States are going through the same kind of denial." Optimists, including Senator Bill Bradley, argue that ultimately America will have no choice but to emerge from its state of denial, that America's leadership will have to accept the fact that the nation cannot thrive if it is torn asunder. "We've got to see diversity as our strength," says Bradley. "We've got to deal with the issue of race. You've got to be candid about it."

To Bradley it's all a matter of common sense, of showing people that "diversity" is not merely an issue of morality but of economic survival: "I do not think people's self interests have been clearly enough and broadly enough defined. . . . Diversity has got to be seen as an economic advantage." Once that happens, argues Bradley, "market forces" will take over, and even social conservatives will come to see that they can ill afford to misuse such a large proportion of the nation's resources.

Francine Soliunas essentially agrees. "I don't think we're going to eliminate racism. But I do think, at least in terms of corporate America, that people are going to recognize that they [cannot] let racism get in the way of the almighty buck. . . . There is a commit-ment to getting rid of anything that is going to interfere with the bottom line. So *something* will be done. Will it be the elimination of racism? I don't think so. But I think there will be enough of a conscious effort to attack some of the qualities that contribute to racism so that it will begin to make people feel that racism itself is being attacked, and to some extent eliminated."

That may be the best that can be expected. Indeed, to ask whether racism can be eliminated or whether it is permanent may be to ask the wrong question. For racism, in some form and to some degree, will always be with us. Daniel Patrick Moynihan makes an important point when he observes that ethnic tension "is so primordial some people argue it's probably genetic. . . . So expect there to be a black/white line; expect there to be a black/white/Asian line. Expect there to be a black Jamaican/black Do-minican/black Mississippian/black born-and-raised-in-the-Bronx-five-centuries line. . . . This is a pattern of behavior."

To say that racism in some form will always be with us, how-ever, is not the same as saying that most people are destined to be racists, or that its most pernicious effects cannot be overcome, or that most blacks in America will always be miserable, or that there is no reason for hope. It is to say that the country has an extremely serious problem—one that it would much rather deny than con-front, much rather wish away than wrestle with honestly—and that vigilance is therefore necessary.

Early in 1993, Major General Wallace C. Arnold, U.S. Army, came to my office at the *Daily News* to solicit the paper's support for the Reserve Officer Training Corps Cadet Command, a pro-gram that tries to instill in high schoolers some sense of leader-ship, self-discipline, and personal responsibility. After he had made his pitch, I asked him a question that had nothing to do with his current mission but had been on my mind since he began talking. Why, I asked him, had the military been so much more successful at providing opportunity for minorities than had the civilian sector?

Without pausing, General Arnold replied, "We've been able to do that because we have a structure . . . in our system to ensure that that has happened." Guidance, he said, was built in, and equal opportunity was enforced. "It's never pushed under the table. It's always placed in front of you." Moreover, "the military is built around teams, and teams, in order to be effective, have to have everybody operating at a competent level. You have to achieve some parity of competence. Competence is recognized. And you have to promote based on competence. . . . Then you give people developmental opportunities. . . . It takes a system to make it happen. And you can't just run it off in little avenues."

The answer was more or less what I had expected. It was the only kind of answer that made any sense: get people to cooperate, to treat each other with respect, and to realize that they have a common interest, then force them to function in a system that recognizes genuine ability and keeps subjective (and potentially career-shattering) assessments to an absolute minimum.

The military, of course, has had more than its share of racial problems, but it has also managed to do a considerably better job than the civilian sector of convincing minorities that they will get a fair shake. That did not happen on its own. It happened in large measure because the military has a structure that can be used, if its leaders so decide, to make people set their prejudices and preconceptions aside.

In the outside world no such neat structure exists. No one is in a position to demand that competence be recognized, cultivated, and rewarded irrespective of skin color—no one, that is, except the very people who have been covering their eyes and ears as they croon, "Wait, give the matter more time. Things are moving along fine. Everything will be as it should in due course. Just be patient."

At Cambridge University, in an address published in the *New York Times Magazine* in 1965, James Baldwin said, "I remember when the ex-Attorney General Mr. Robert Kennedy said it was conceivable that in forty years in America we might have a Negro President. That sounded like a very emancipated statement to white people. They were not in Harlem when this statement was first heard. They did not hear the laughter and the bitterness and scorn with which this statement was greeted. From the point of view of the man in the Harlem barber shop, Bobby Kennedy only got here yesterday and now he is already on his way to the Presidency. We were here for four hundred years and now he tells us that maybe in forty years, if you are good, we may let you become President.''

If there was one sentiment that consistently came through in interview after interview with very successful black people in all walks of life, it can be summed up in one phrase: *We are tired of waiting.*

chapter nine *No More White Guilt*

$\mathcal{S}$EVERAL YEARS AGO, DISCUSSING LAWSUITS brought against her paper by minorities and women's groups in the 1970s, the *New York Times* legal counsel told me, "I always felt in the women's case that it was like a divorce or a custody proceeding. . . . There wasn't any of that in the minorities case. And I suppose it's for a very simple reason. There were so few minorities, so few longstanding preexisting relationships, you didn't have the sense of a family being rent asunder. The gap was too wide."

The gap was too wide. The phrase has stayed with me, for it seems to sum up the situation not only at the *New York Times* but across much of America, where whites and minorities—blacks, in particular—stare at each other across a vast (and at points seemingly unbridgeable) chasm. We have become so accustomed to the estrangement that it generally doesn't strike us as strange. As the *Times* executive observed, it is not a rupture between family members but between people who can barely conceive of themselves as belonging to the same tribe or sharing a common heritage. Yet occasionally something happens that makes it clear that this estrangement, however entrenched, is not particularly healthy—at least not for a nation that purports to believe that justice and opportunity should be color-blind.

Through much of 1992 and 1993, many Americans sat before their television sets engrossed in the saga of Rodney King. The videotaped beating, the riot in Los Angeles, and the two trials of the cops who pummeled King into submission provided any num-

ber of irresistible television moments; but they also did something
more. They forced America to focus, at least briefly, on the problems of racial hostility and interracial alienation. And they high-
lighted the fact that despite the progress of the past few years,
blacks and whites of all social and economic classes still sometimes see the same events in extremely different ways.

Certainly, in a literal sense, blacks and whites saw the same
thing: a group of white policemen who repeatedly struck and
backed away from the semiprone figure of King. That image was
sufficiently powerful and unsettling that people of all races were
sickened by it. Yet most whites viewed the beating as a shocking
but isolated incident. Indeed, it was so stunning, at least in part,
because it was taken to be so unusual. For most blacks, it was
confirmation that a brutality many had experienced firsthand reflected a broader problem of brutality and race-based inequity
within the criminal justice system.

"In the days after the acquittal of four white Los Angeles police
officers charged in the beating of a black man, black and white
opinions were uncharacteristically in synch on a racial question,"
wrote *Washington Post* reporter Lynne Duke in June 1992.
"Large majorities of whites and overwhelming majorities of
blacks told pollsters that the verdict was wrong. . . . But when
asked if the verdict 'shows that blacks cannot get justice in this
country,' black and white opinion hit a fork in the road: 78 percent of blacks said yes, compared with only 25 percent of whites."

The following year, during the second trial of the accused policemen, Bobby Doctor, acting director of the U.S. Civil Rights
Commission, told me he had witnessed a number of police beatings during his civil rights work in the South. He said that he and
other prominent African Americans had long spoken out against
police brutality—"but nobody's been listening." With the Rodney
King video, "finally, it was there for the country to see, for the
world to see."

Wade Henderson, director of the Washington office of the
NAACP, also sees King's ordeal as representing much more than
the tribulations of one man. He described King as "a black Every-
man whose experience with police came to symbolize African-

American encounters with law enforcement.'' Not that King was anyone's idea of a model citizen. He was an ex-con with a penchant for drinking and trouble—hardly a typical, hardworking black American. Many African Americans nonetheless identified strongly with King—not because of who he was but because of what he had been through. No matter whose account of that night in the San Fernando Valley is accepted, no matter what motivation is attributed to the police, King was dealt with, to use Henderson's words, ''as something other than a man.'' In *Presumed Guilty*, his book about the Rodney King encounter, Stacey Koon, the police sergeant in charge at the scene, depicts King as a ''huge guy'' possessing ''superhuman strength'' who was completely oblivious to pain. This language strikes Henderson as having less to do with reality than with dehumanizing stereotypes of the sort African Americans have routinely encountered in dealing with law enforcement officers. Many blacks who put themselves in King's place saw him not as a bum who had received rough treatment but as ''a glaring reminder that being black in America means that you operate under a different set of rules,'' as Henderson puts it.

The discrepancy in black and white reactions to the King beating is certainly not surprising. As we have seen, the polling literature is replete with examples of blacks and whites in fundamental disagreement over the most basic facts of American life. In their 1992 survey of Los Angeles County, for instance, researchers at UCLA's Center for the Study of Urban Poverty found that 60 percent of blacks had ''not much'' confidence in the police, while only 16 percent of whites felt similarly. Eighty percent of blacks agreed with the statement that ''blacks usually don't get fair treatment in the courts and criminal justice system,'' compared to 40 percent of whites. And three-fourths of blacks felt that ''American society owes people of my ethnic group a better chance in life than we currently have.''

As the astonished UCLA researchers discovered, economic success is no remedy for despair over what blacks perceive as deeply rooted racial inequities. *But why should that be?* Why shouldn't blacks who are affluent, well-educated, and blessed by life acknowledge their good fortune and be content? Why should blacks making six- and seven-figure incomes identify at all with the likes of Rodney King?

Part of the answer lies in David Dinkins's epigram: "A white man with a million dollars is a millionaire, and a black man with a million dollars is a nigger with a million dollars." His obvious point is that many whites have great difficulty differentiating a black go-getter from a black bum, that at night on a lonely stretch of highway a malicious cop is as likely to bash one black head as another. And even if Dinkins doesn't believe his own words, plenty of other blacks do—or at least believe that countless cops see color first and class later, if at all.

Certainly, as police sergeant Don Jackson confirmed during his self-assigned undercover foray into Long Beach, a black skin, in and of itself, can arouse a dangerous degree of suspicion. Numerous others have discovered the same thing. In Reynoldsburg, Ohio, for example, the NAACP claimed that racial hostility was so unrestrained that the police had organized a SNAT—Special Nigger Arrest Team—for the express purpose of harassing blacks. For many black Americans, police abuse is an old story, at least as old as the battle for civil rights. And though the nation was stunned by the police treatment of Rodney King, and even more so by the terrifying riot that followed the acquittal of his assailants, it's worth recalling that this was far from the first instance of conflict between a minority community and the police. Most of the riots of the 1960s were ignited by similar episodes. In 1980, a devastating riot swept Miami when an all-white jury exonerated several white policemen accused of viciously beating a black man following a high-speed chase. Unlike King, Arthur McDuffie died from his injuries. Unlike King, McDuffie, an insurance executive, was a bona fide member of the middle class.

Much of the history of blacks in America is a history of mistreatment and harassment by agents of the state. The so-called Ku Klux Klan Acts, passed by Congress during Reconstruction, were aimed specifically at law enforcement officers who denied newly enfranchised blacks their rights; and though those laws are well over a century old, the U.S. Justice Department continues to find cases that justify their use. Small wonder, then, that in many minority communities reports of police brutality are granted instant (and sometimes unmerited) credibility.

Yet for all the symbolic significance of such cases, it is not thoughts of McDuffie, King, and other African Americans victimized by cops that keep black professionals awake at night. The rage of the black middle class can hardly be laid at the feet of the police. As awful as Rodney King's treatment may have been, most middle-class blacks know that they are not very likely to find themselves on the wrong side of a policeman's baton.

The source of their outrage is generally much more prosaic: a colleague, clerk, or prospective neighbor—someone whose only weapons are words and disapproval, and who causes great pain while truly intending no harm. When the senior partner in the big law firm goes to a store and is treated "like I make two cents and am uneducated," he is in exactly the same boat as Dinkins's "nigger with a million dollars." When an accomplished jurist complains of white counterparts who "want you to do well, but not *that* well" and wonders what he might have achieved had he really "been given a fair shot," he is making the same point: that the benefits of material success do not include exemption from being treated as a "nigger." When University of Illinois sociologist Sharon Collins asks whether it is possible for a black person to make race not matter, she is saying, along with the vast majority of other black professionals I interviewed, that America is not nearly as free as it thinks it is of the bigotry that defined its past.

As I write this, the local New York press is reporting on a new study by a Queens College professor showing that blacks in the city, at all income levels, remain extremely segregated from other groups. On my desk sits a huge binder of papers delivered at the 1992 housing conference of the Federal National Mortgage Association (Fannie Mae), reviewing several years of research documenting discrimination encountered by blacks and Hispanic Americans in the housing market. The authors of several of the papers note that when black and Hispanic auditors go into predominantly white areas in search of housing, they are routinely steered into neighborhoods that have more minorities. Other papers focus on trends in lending institutions and on evidence indicating that blacks, whatever their economic profile, have more difficulty getting mortgages than whites. John Kain, a professor of economic and Afro-American studies at Harvard University, offers his opinion (disputed by some other researchers) that "the restriction of black households to massive central-city ghettos, and a few small and isolated black communities located elsewhere in the metropolitan area," denies many African Americans information about and access to jobs and high-quality schools. Anthony Downs, an economist with the Brookings Institution, observes, "Racial and ethnic discrimination is so widespread and has persisted so long in American housing markets that it must be supported by powerful motives and incentives."

Perusing the collection of academic housing studies takes me back to my own first experience looking for an apartment outside of Chicago's black neighborhoods. The tenant of a two-bedroom flat in a trendy North Side area had placed an ad seeking someone to sublet. When I called, her manner was cordial and gregarious; when I arrived a few hours later, she was still polite but decidedly more reserved. She hastily pointed out a few of the apartment's attractions and then excused herself to make a call from the bedroom. It soon became clear that she was talking to the landlord, for in a whisper that I clearly was not supposed to hear, she confided to the person on the other end that a well-dressed black man had answered the ad. Was it all right, she wondered, to show the apartment? The owner, who I later discovered had a black girlfriend, apparently allayed her concerns. The woman returned to the living room with a smile on her face and proceeded to show me around.

My application for the apartment was approved without incident. Still, the woman's behavior made a powerful and unambiguous point: that though the apartment was for rent, it might not be available to someone of my race. And angered as I was at the thought that she—or anyone else—would presume to judge and perhaps reject me simply because of my color, I meekly accepted the treatment as the price to be paid for looking where *my kind* was deemed not to belong.

In *American Apartheid*, sociologists Douglass Massey and

Nancy Denton catalogue a multitude of evils tied to racial segregation in housing. Like Harvard's John Kain, they blame it for barring blacks from many jobs and schools, but their indictment goes much further. Segregation isolates blacks politically, they charge, and is responsible for the development of an "oppositional culture" in which "a majority of children are born out of wedlock, . . . most families are on welfare, . . . educational failure prevails, and . . . social and physical deterioration abound." In short, they blame segregation for the existence of a black underclass, and they argue that its deleterious effects are not limited to poor blacks.

"Middle-class households—whether they are black, Mexican, Italian, Jewish, or Polish—always try to escape the poor," they point out. "But only blacks must attempt their escape within a highly segregated, racially segmented housing market. Because of segregation, middle-class blacks are less able to escape than other groups, and as a result are exposed to more poverty. At the same time, because of segregation no one will move into a poor black neighborhood except other poor blacks. Thus both middle-class and poor blacks lose compared with the poor and middle class of other groups: poor blacks live under unrivaled concentrations of poverty and affluent blacks live in neighborhoods that are far less advantageous than those experienced by the middle class of other groups."

The pervasiveness of segregation in America's large cities is beyond dispute, as is the wickedness of a system that exhorts blacks to escape the ghetto and its associated pathologies and then batters them for trying. And as noted in previous chapters, even blacks who do manage to "escape" often encounter problems of another sort. The anger of black suburbanites who are never invited to join private clubs near their homes and the anxiety of black parents trying to raise children in communities where they feel socially isolated say volumes about how pernicious old attitudes can be. And even if residential segregation could be eliminated (which seems an unlikely proposition for the near future), what is to be done about psychological segregation—about the tendency of Americans to force each other into comfortable, separate and racially stereotypical pigeonholes?

The pain of the professionals profiled in the preceding pages is more often than not rooted in feelings of exclusion. In attempting to escape that pain, some blacks end up, in effect, inviting increased isolation. When the successful black lawyer declares that he will "go to my own people for acceptance" because he no longer expects approbation from whites, he is not only expressing solidarity with other members of his race, he is also conceding defeat. He is saying that he is giving up hope of ever being anything but a talented "nigger" to many of his white colleagues, that he refuses to invest emotionally in those who will never quite see him as one of them, whatever his personal and professional attributes.

His white peers would of course be shocked to discover that he finds his workplace a hostile environment and that he feels a need to protect himself from them emotionally. *What,* they would wonder, *can be his problem?* Just as white students on so many college campuses wonder why so many of their black counterparts huddle together adamantly refusing to join "the mainstream."

Whites often take such behavior as a manifestation of irrational antiwhite prejudice. But in most cases, it is perhaps better understood as a reaction similar to that of the lawyer above—as a retreat from a "mainstream" they have come to feel is an irremediably hostile place. Some people would say that they are flat-out wrong, that for blacks willing to meet whites halfway, race no longer has to matter, at least not all that much.

Yet pretending (or convincing ourselves) that race no longer matters (or wouldn't if minorities stopped demanding special treatment) is not quite the same as making it not matter. Creating a color-blind society on a foundation saturated with the venom of racism requires something more than simply proclaiming that the age of brotherhood has arrived. Somehow, as America went from a country concerned about denial of civil rights to one obsessed with "reverse racism" and "quotas" that discriminate against white males, some important steps were missed. Among other things, we neglected as a nation to make any serious attempt to understand why, if racial conditions were improving so much, legions of those who should be celebrating were still singing the blues. To answer that question would have meant, at a minimum, truly listening to what the dissatisfied were saying instead of writing them off as unreasonable whiners.

In summing up the problems of Brooklyn's Crown Heights community, Ed Koch made a telling point. "The Jews feel beleaguered and angry . . . because they're the only white group that stayed. You can't find white groups remaining in areas where blacks move in and become the dominant group. Whites move out. The Jews stayed and they think maybe the city ought to give them a little credit for that, including the black community." *Why*, I wondered as he talked, *should any group get special credit for not maniacally shunning blacks?* What kind of society have we created in which it is considered acceptable to flee entire communities merely because members of another race move in?

Years ago, a very close white friend of mine was stabbed by a black stranger on a city street. The attack nearly killed her, and she spent several weeks in a hospital recovering from her wound. Despite her terrible ordeal, she managed to maintain a cheery outward disposition and continued to exhibit an amazing generosity of spirit. Her friends, of course, were delighted at her recovery, and at her ability to accept her misfortune with grace. At least one friend was also surprised that she emerged with no apparent aversion to blacks. "Isn't it wonderful," the woman remarked, "that after all she has been through, she doesn't hate black people?"

I had assumed that my wounded friend would regard her assailant as a depraved individual, not as a representative of the entire black race, and therefore found the rhetorical question peculiar. I could not get it out of my head. For the woman was essentially saying that my friend deserved special credit for being able to treat black people as individuals, as *human beings*.

Maybe she did deserve special credit for not hating blacks. And maybe the Jews of Crown Heights deserve accolades for staying in the neighborhood. But what kind of values are we promoting if we praise people solely because they choose not to treat African Americans like "niggers"? Are we saying that anyone more tolerant than Archie Bunker is a great humanitarian by our standards? Are we insinuating that real racial harmony is so unnatural or so difficult to achieve that we might as well settle for an uneasy and unequal coexistence?

This is not quite the dream that motivated and sustained the civil rights movement, the dream for which people of all races marched, were manhandled, and in some cases died. But it may be all that many Americans at present are willing to countenance.

And what, one might ask, is so bad about that? It is not as if no progress has been made. By any reasonable criteria, African Americans, at least those who are well educated and enterprising, have more opportunities than ever. Despite the bellyaching of well-to-do blacks, many are doing much better than most whites. In a world where no one is guaranteed success or even a fair shake, shouldn't the well-documented stereotype-shattering triumphs of the black middle class be more than enough to satisfy anyone?

Moreover, doesn't this country have more pressing problems than the complaints of affluent blacks unwilling to accept a few race-related inconveniences? And don't whites have problems too? Don't struggling whites—even if they are male—deserve a little sympathy? Isn't there an inequality of compassion here? As my impassioned, if impolitic, correspondent asked, "Why is it always racism when a black person is called nigger, but not when a white person is called a white bitch?" Life is rough for a lot of people, not all of whom are black. So why, given the advantages at least some African Americans so conspicuously enjoy, should whites feel any guilt whatsoever?

To an increasing number of whites, that question seems less and less outrageous. And that may not be entirely bad. It would probably be healthier for all concerned if the current dialogue about racial justice focused much less than it has thus far on issues of guilt and victimization. Making someone feel sorry for you, after all, is not the same as getting them to recognize you as an equal—or even as a human being. At most, it provides a foundation for charity, or for what is perceived as charity—for which one is expected to be appropriately grateful, even if what is offered is not what one needs or feels one deserves.

A black director of a large bank told me of a board meeting he attended at which evidence was presented that the bank was not treating its black customers the same way it treated whites. Blacks with equivalent earnings and credit histories had significantly lower loan approval rates. The directors recognized immediately that they had a problem, that it was clear they had to do a much better job with "affirmative action." One board member bluntly disagreed, pointing out that the problem had nothing to do with affirmative action, that the bank was simply not acting in its own best interest in rejecting loans that should be approved. The black director was grateful for his colleague's intervention, for he had often seen such statements go unchallenged. The first inclination of some of his fellow board members was to consider initiatives that might benefit blacks as something other than normal business, something that belonged in the category of charity and good works. Thus, the directors could give themselves special credit for doing what was right by any standard.

It may very well be that the civil rights debate has been so distorted by strategies designed to engender guilt that many whites, as a form of self-defense, have come to define any act of decency toward blacks as an act of expiation. If an end to such strategies—and indeed an end to white guilt—would result in a more intelligent racial dialogue, I, for one, am all for wiping the slate clean. The problem is certainly not that people do not feel guilty enough; it is that so many are in denial. And though denial may be a great way to avoid an unpleasant reality, it is no substitute for changing that reality. Nor, more to the point, will it do much to narrow the huge chasm that separates so many blacks and whites.

The racial gap, as this book has tried to make clear, can only be closed by recognizing it, and by recognizing why it exists. That will not come to pass as long as we insist on dividing people into different camps and then swearing that differences don't count or that repeated blows to the soul shouldn't be taken seriously. For the truth is that the often hurtful and seemingly trivial encounters of daily existence are in the end what most of life is.